T0328586

Cambridge Elements ≡

Elements in Metaphysics
edited by
Tuomas E. Tahko
University of Bristol

GROUNDING, FUNDAMENTALITY AND ULTIMATE EXPLANATIONS

Ricki Bliss
Lehigh University

Shaftesbury Road, Cambridge CB2 8EA, United Kingdom

One Liberty Plaza, 20th Floor, New York, NY 10006, USA

477 Williamstown Road, Port Melbourne, VIC 3207, Australia

314–321, 3rd Floor, Plot 3, Splendor Forum, Jasola District Centre, New Delhi – 110025, India

103 Penang Road, #05–06/07, Visioncrest Commercial, Singapore 238467

Cambridge University Press is part of Cambridge University Press & Assessment, a department of the University of Cambridge.

We share the University's mission to contribute to society through the pursuit of education, learning and research at the highest international levels of excellence.

www.cambridge.org
Information on this title: www.cambridge.org/9781009479394

DOI: 10.1017/9781009089739

First published 2024

A catalogue record for this publication is available from the British Library.

ISBN 978-1-009-47939-4 Hardback
ISBN 978-1-009-09637-9 Paperback
ISSN 2633-9862 (online)
ISSN 2633-9854 (print)

Grounding, Fundamentality and Ultimate Explanations

Elements in Metaphysics

DOI: 10.1017/9781009089739
First published online: March 2024

Ricki Bliss
Lehigh University
Author for correspondence: Ricki Bliss, rickibliss@gmail.com

Abstract: There is a long lineage of philosophers concerned with coming to understand what explains everything broadly construed, or within a certain, restricted domain. We call such explanations *ultimate explanations*. Contemporarily, philosophers of a certain stripe have devoted much attention to the notion of *fundamentality* – that there is something which is without explanation. This Element explores some of the connections between fundamentality and ultimate explanations both contemporarily and historically.

Keywords: grounding, fundamentality, ultimate explanations, metaphysical foundationalism

ISBNs: 9781009479394 (HB), 9781009096379 (PB), 9781009089739 (OC)
ISSNs: 2633-9862 (online), 2633-9854 (print)

Contents

Introduction   1

1 Groundwork: Grounding and Fundamentality   3

2 Ultimate Explanations: An Idea and Its History   18

3 The Metaphysics of Fundamentality   34

4 The Epistemology of Fundamentality: Regresses, Virtues
  and Other Desiderata   42

5 Fundamentality: Some Misgivings and Its Alternatives   51

References   68

Introduction

In the last few decades, big picture metaphysics has enjoyed something of a renaissance in certain corners of the philosophical universe. One might opine that big picture metaphysics has *always* been the business that metaphysicians are in – what is thinking about causation or the nature of time, for example, if not engaging in big picture metaphysics? Point taken. Perhaps it is more accurate to say, then, that a *certain kind* of big picture metaphysics has been back in vogue. The first feature of this approach to metaphysics is that it is preoccupied with treating issues surrounding the overarching structure of reality. It is not so much concerned with what the relation is between, say, a member and its set or the table and its parts *only*, but, rather, how members, sets, tables and table parts fit into a broader order of things. In particular, a whole branch of metaphysics has sprouted around the idea that reality has a distinctively *non-causal* overarching structure and that this structure is fixed by relations of *ground*.

In addition to the exploitation of the notion of ground, the strain of contemporary metaphysics that I have in mind appears also to be in the business of engaging with old school, big picture kinds of questions. Although this point is often not made as explicitly as I believe it ought to be, a lot of contemporary metaphysics has been preoccupied with questions such as 'what explains the nature and existence of everything?' It is as a result of attempting to respond to questions surrounding the ultimate nature and structure of the cosmos – or perhaps just some corner of it – that we have seen a lot of attention paid to the idea that there is something *fundamental*. Commonly coupled with kinds of naturalism or physicalism, the idea that there is something fundamental, that it is physical and that this fundamental physical stuff (and I use 'stuff' here in a non-metaphysically loaded way) accounts for the rest of the physical universe, at least, has become fairly mainstream. A final feature of the kind of metaphysics that I have in mind is that these kinds of questions, this approach to metaphysics, takes the issues with which it is concerned at face value. Questions about the overarching structure of reality are questions about mind-independent reality; they are not to be palmed off as the result of linguistic tangles or conceptual confusions. Questions about what grounds what are questions about the world out there.

This kind of big picture metaphysics – the kind that is preoccupied with notions of grounding and fundamentality – is what this Element is about. In particular, it is focused on how contemporary thinkers have been thinking about fundamentality, and how the notion of ground is used in service to that. But this Element is not just about how contemporary thinkers have been thinking about fundamentality. It also takes seriously the idea that many philosophers across time, geographical location and tradition have also been in the business of thinking about the (non-causal) overarching structure of reality and what is fundamental.

In this Element, I assume – an assumption that I defend in Section 2 – that we can reasonably suppose that historic figures have also been in the business of understanding the broader, non-causal structure of reality and what ultimately explains it. One reason to suppose that historic figures don't, in fact, make use of the notion of grounding is that statements of ground involve claims about a relationship between facts or propositions and most historical figures didn't talk in this way. Heidegger, for example, didn't claim that the fact that Being is grounds the fact that beings are – or something of the like.[1] Instead, we might understand him as having made claims about Being grounding beings; so, claims about *things* grounding *things*.[2] Some contemporaries are happy to understand grounding as holding between things.[3] Others are of the view that grounding links propositions or fact-like entities. I will oftentimes speak most generally in the language of *entities* as involved with grounding. Not only will this allow me to be ecumenical as regards the many views about the nature of grounding, but it also allows me to speak about historic Western and non-Western views that were not formulated in the language of facts.

This Element offers an, albeit brief, overview of the notion of fundamentality. In Section 1, I introduce the notions of grounding and fundamentality. In Section 2, I defend the thought that neither grounding nor fundamentality are new. In Section 3, I offer a discussion of some aspects of the metaphysics of fundamentality before turning, in Section 4, to its epistemology. In the final section, Section 5, I introduce some alternative views. I, along with others, have defended the possibility of these alternative views, as well as having drawn attention to the prevalence of these alternative views in non-Western traditions. It has not been uncommon for philosophers in the contemporary discussion, on the one hand, to assume that fundamentality is roughly correct and, on the other hand, to appeal to something like an intuition for assuming that to be the case. I now think that such an attitude has actually made foundationalism an easy target, and that there are powerful arguments that speak to the strength of the

---

[1] I am aware that even if Heidegger had spoken in the language of facts, he wouldn't have been able to formulate a grounding claim like this. My example here is just to highlight a point about fact – versus thing – talk in historic figures.

[2] Again, I am aware that it is controversial to claim that for Heidegger Being is a thing. I am not intending to make a substantive claim about the metaphysics of Being for Heidegger, but rather a point about grounding being used in a way such that it doesn't connect propositions or fact-like entities. I hope the reader can understand my claim here charitably. See Casati (2021).

[3] See, for example, Schaffer (2009).

view. This is not to say that I now think that foundationalism is correct, but that it is much more compelling and much harder to dislodge than I once thought.

1 Groundwork: Grounding and Fundamentality

The world contains many and varied things: trumpets, numbers, sentences, facts, wars and great disappointments. These things – let us call them the constituents of the world or entities – enter into relationships with other of the world's constituents. Trumpets are (type-)identical to other trumpets, for example, and wars tend to be the cause of many great disappointments. Amongst the relations of metaphysical importance that lend structure to the shape of our world are also relations that we call *grounding relations*.

What does it mean to say that one thing grounds another? Matters here, as we shall see, are complicated, but let us begin with some (allegedly) intuitive examples. Take a trumpet. Whilst that trumpet was caused to be through the activity of an instrument maker, it bears a particularly important relationship to its parts. We can say, then, that the existence of the trumpet is grounded in the existence of its parts. Turning to the consideration of war, history books are filled with tales of what caused various wars to happen: Franz Ferdinand was assassinated, Hitler invaded Poland, terrorists attacked the World Trade Center on September the 11th. But just as trumpets seem to bear an important, non-causal relationship to their parts, wars seem to bear an important non-causal relationship to the events that constitute them. Regardless of what caused a war to begin, what it is to be a war – perhaps a particular war – is to have troops massed at a border, economic relations severed or leaders pointing nuclear weapons at each other's nations. These events that are constitutive of a state of war can be said to ground the event that is that war.

Grounding relations need not obtain exclusively between concrete, contingent entities. For the structuralist about numbers, for example, the identity of, say, the number 7 will be grounded in the mathematical structures it is embedded in. Consider, now, the proposition <all people have a heart>. Understood as a universal generalization, the truth of this proposition will be grounded in the truth of its particular instances – <Sally has a heart>, <Pete has a heart> and so on.

From here, it seems like we can already say several things about the notion of grounding. First, grounding seems to be a distinctively non-causal kind of metaphysical relation. Second, grounding relations seem to obtain between entities of a variety of (possibly all) categories. Third, grounding looks to be familiar. That wholes bear an important relationship to their parts or that events are comprised of events is by no means a recent or even striking discovery.

Fourth, the relation looks to induce a kind of hierarchy. Something like intuition tells us that if the trumpet is grounded in its parts, then the parts aren't also grounded in the trumpet. Fifth, grounding seems to be intimately involved with a certain kind of (non-causal) explanation.

Unfortunately, however, here we are already flirting with controversy, as there is very, very little that proponents of grounding agree upon. In the coming pages, we will ride roughshod over many of the issues central to coming to understand the notion of grounding that friend and foe of the notion alike disagree upon.

1.1 Grounding: The Framework and Some of Its Controversies

Discussions of grounding generally start with a slew of example cases of the phenomenon that are widely assumed to be intuitive or obvious. The existence of wholes is grounded in the existence of their parts, the existence of sets is grounded in their members and the truth of certain kinds of propositions is grounded in the truth of certain other kinds of propositions as determined by the laws of logic. But, agreeing upon such example cases, very little, it turns out, has been settled.

1.1.1 The Relata

So far, I have made claims such as 'the war is grounded in the events that constitute it' and 'the existence of the trumpet is grounded in the existence of its parts'. What, then, are the relata of grounding relations? According to one view, the relata of grounding relations can be drawn from any and all ontological categories and the relation can obtain cross-categorically.[4] On such an approach, it is perfectly acceptable to claim that a trumpet is grounded in its parts, that a fact is grounded in its (non-facty) constituents, that an event is grounded in other events or that a truth is grounded in its truth-maker (a piece of the world). Assuming that 'entity' is the broadest ontological term available, we can refer to this kind of approach as *entity-grounding*.

The alternative, and more popular, view denies that grounding can obtain between relata of all categories or cross-categorically and, instead, holds that the only relata apt to enter into grounding relations are relata that have a propositional structure.[5] On some views, this will be tantamount to saying that grounding relations obtain between worldly entities like facts. Consider, again, how some of our grounding claims have been phrased earlier – 'the existence of the parts ground the existence of the whole'. As a statement of

---

[4] See, for example, Schaffer (2009).
[5] See, for example, deRossett (2013), Fine (2012) and Rosen (2010).

ground, this sentence looks to express a relationship not between things – parts and wholes – but between entities with a propositional structure – <the existence of the parts> and <the existence of a whole>. Recognizing that we have said nothing yet as regards the relationship between sentences, propositions and facts, let us call this second approach *propositional-grounding*.

As we shall come to see, philosophers who can be considered proponents of the propositional approach nonetheless disagree over what the relata of grounding relations are. Some are of the view that the relata are *facts*, whereas others are of the view that grounding talk is best understood in terms of connectives between *sentences*.[6] Why one of these views might be preferable to the other, we shall come to in a moment, but let us first consider why one might prefer one of entity- or propositional-grounding over the other.

Entity-grounding not only looks to have historical precedent, but it also has a certain kind of intuitive appeal that speaks in its favour. One way of understanding the relationship between Being and entities (beings) in Heidegger, for example, is in terms of the notion of grounding: Being grounds entities.[7] In this particular case, not only is the relationship not typically expressed as one that obtains between propositional entities, but there is good reason to think it cannot be. For Heidegger, exactly what Being cannot do is *be*, in which case claims such as 'the being of Being grounds the being of beings' don't work. It is Being that grounds beings and not the being of that Being. It is not hard to uncover many cases in which a grounding relationship appears to be expressed in this way. We say that sets are grounded in their members, or that God grounds everything else. But, thinks the proponent of propositional-grounding, although we may *say* that sets are grounded in their members or that God grounds everything, things – sets, God – don't actually ground anything. When we say that a set is grounded in its members, what we really mean to say is that the fact that the set exists is grounded in the fact that its members exist, or something of the like. Sets, Gods, numbers or wars don't ground, or aren't grounded by, anything. It's their having of a certain feature that stands in need of grounding and their having a certain feature that does that grounding work. Or so the reasoning goes. That this is the way grounding behaves, thinks the proponent of the propositional account, is the reason that they prefer this account.

What the propositional account is highly suggestive of is a tight and important connection between grounding and explanation. In fact, it is not uncommon to hear it said that grounding just is *metaphysical explanation*. Putting aside how we might understand the exact connection between grounding and

---

[6] See for example Rosen (2010) as an example of the former and Fine (2012) as an example of the latter.

[7] Casati (2019) and (2021).

explanation, it is not difficult to see why philosophers might think both that there is an important connection and that grounding ought to be understood propositionally. Look, again, to some examples of grounding statements: 'the table exists because its parts exist and are arranged thus and such a way', 'The United Kingdom is a constitutional monarchy in virtue of having both a king and a parliamentary system'. In both cases, we have sentential connectives – 'in virtue of' and 'because' – that express a relation of ground. And in both cases the statement of ground has a propositional structure that also conveys an explanatory connection. What explains the fact that the United Kingdom is a constitutional monarchy is the fact that it has a king as well as a parliamentary system. What explains the existence of the table is the existence and arrangement of its parts. Strictly speaking, tables and kings don't explain anything. What does explain things, however, is the *existence* of a king and the *having* of a parliamentary system.

1.1.2 The Relation

Just as philosophers disagree over what the relata of the grounding relation are, they also disagree over how we are to best understand the relation. Indeed, there is disagreement over whether statements of ground express a relation at all. Disputes over how best to understand this central cluster of issues range over two main concerns: (1) is grounding best expressed by a sentential connective or a relational predicate, and (2) is grounding just metaphysical explanation or does it merely underwrite or back it?

Let us consider first the debate between proponents of the sentential connective approach and proponents of the relational predicate approach. According to the former – the sentential connective approach – statements such as 'the table exists because its parts exist', or 'justice prevails in virtue of truth', can be understood in the same way we understand sentences such as 'the building is sleek and modern'. We have a connective – in our case 'because'/'in virtue of' – that joins two sentences to form a sentence, in much the same way that 'and' connects sentences to form other sentences. The sentential connective approach understands grounding claims without insisting that there are worldly relations or the worldly entities that those relations relate. That the sentential connective approach is not metaphysically loaded in this way is often cited as one big reason that speaks in its favour.

In contrast, the relational predicate approach is ontologically committing. According to this view, statements such as 'the building is tall and sleek in virtue of its being tall and its being sleek' or 'the existence of the table is grounded in the existence of its parts' employ a relational predicate, *grounds*, that picks out a real relation of ground. What this relation is thought to relate is commonly propositions or facts. This view, then, moves us from sentences to worldly entities – grounding relations and facts. Taking the sentence 'the existence of the table is grounded in the existence of its parts' on the relational predicate approach delivers the result that what the grounding claim conveys is that the fact that the table exists is grounded in the fact that its parts exist – two facts related by a grounding relation. To be clear, though, all the relational predicate approach commits us to, strictly speaking, is the existence of a worldly grounding relation. It is still open to the proponent of this approach to claim that the relata that flank the relation can be, say, things as opposed to facts. Although the relational predicate approach is ontologically committing, many are happy to pay this price. For anyone of a realist bent, that the claims pick out a worldly relation is natural and desirable.

The second dimension along which there is disagreement over how we are to understand grounding pertains to its relationship to metaphysical explanation. According to *unionists*, grounding just *is* metaphysical explanation. According to the *separatists*, on the other hand, grounding relations underwrite metaphysical explanations and are not, therewith, identical to them.[8] Matters here are complicated and made all the more so by the fact that the relationship between grounding and explanation is often taken for granted and its nuances often not explicitly stated or even recognized.

Why prefer one approach over the other? Insight into the nature of ground, it is commonly believed, is to be achieved by way of an examination of explanation. It is by looking at the better understood notion of explanation that we can come to learn how grounding behaves; and by looking to explanation that we come to be able to justify positing a relation of grounding in the first place.[9] One reason to prefer the unionist approach is that it is simpler. Instead of having two phenomena – grounding and explanation – and two phenomena whose relationship to one another then also needs to be accounted for, we can claim that grounding just is explanation and be done with it. And this is easy enough as grounding behaves remarkably like explanation anyway: it is asymmetric, transitive, irreflexive, non-monotonic and hyperintensional. What the discovery of grounding-as-synonymous-with-explanation has allowed us to do is to recognize that there is a distinctively non-causal mode of explanation that is familiar to us from domains as varied as the special sciences, ethics and

---

[8] See Raven (2015), Maurin (2019) and Brenner et al. (2021).

[9] See Maurin (2019) for a thorough discussion of the relationship between grounding and explanation as it is widely understood in the literature; as well as a discussion of the many problems with the extant views.

everyday explanatory contexts.[10]

The unionist approach is not without its problems, however. Primary amongst them is that grounding is widely believed to be objective and mind-independent, whereas explanation is thought to be inextricably tied up in our cognitive lives. Even on accounts according to which explanation is objective, it is nonetheless undeniably tied up with the understanding and the aim of increasing it. If mind-independent grounding just is mind-dependent explanation, then the unionist view appears to have a serious tension at its heart.[11]

This leaves us, then, with separatism, according to which relations of ground merely back or underwrite metaphysical explanations. What speaks in favour of this view? One big advantage of separatism is that it accommodates the views both that grounding is mind-independent and that explanations are not. Grounding relations are worldly entities that, in some important sense, make certain explanatory claims true: it is because the world has thus and such a metaphysical structure that certain kinds of explanations are true. It is because singleton Socrates is grounded in Socrates that we can say that the existence of Socrates metaphysically explains the existence of his singleton. We can still comfortably claim that because of the tight connection between grounding and metaphysical explanation, we can learn much about the nature of the former from looking to the latter, but we are not forced to collapse the two into one another. One problem for this view, however – the avoidance of which is already mentioned as a distinct advantage of unionism – is that in positing two different kinds of things, grounding relations and metaphysical explanations, we now need to say something about how the two are related: what kind of relation is this backing relation? If it's a kind of grounding relation, then the view looks unstable. After all, if we are invoking explanation to understand grounding, it seems dangerously close to begging the question to need to appeal to grounding to make sense of how the explanation that we are employing to understand grounding requires an understanding of grounding in the first place. And if it's not a kind of grounding relation, then we need to know what kind of relation we are dealing with.

1.1.3 Further Important Features

In spite of the many sources of disagreement, at this point the reader should begin to have a clearer sense of what philosophers have in mind when speaking about the notion of ground and why it might be important. Grounding is

---

[10] See Miller and Morton (2022).

[11] It is not clear, either, that potential ways of resolving this tension work. We could admit, for example, that there is such a thing as mind-independent explanation, but it is hard to understand what explanation so conceived could be like. See Maurin (2019) for discussion.

intimately involved with metaphysical explanation and the task of elucidating the overarching structure of reality. Speaking in such terms – in terms of the overarching structure of reality – there is a further important feature of the notion of ground deserving of our attention.

Is there a generic relation of ground that orders the contents of reality into a superstructure or are we to understand the notion of ground as something like a covering term that picks out specific kinds of grounding relations that lend structure without inducing an overarching, all-inclusive shape? There are two separate clusters of issues that intersect here. First, there is the conceptual question of how the notion of grounding stands to the relations that are so often wheeled out as examples of it – parthood and membership, for example. Second, there is the metaphysical question of how reality is arranged once we have a certain understanding of grounding operating in the background. One might think, for example, that there is no overarching ordering, but rather a series of orderings relativized to different ordering relations. I discuss these two sets of issues in their turn.

Recall, again, some of the grounding claims presented earlier – the existence of the table is grounded in the existence of its parts; singleton Socrates exists because Socrates exists. In both cases the relationships are presented in the language of grounding, but in both cases, we are also aware that there is an additional relation in operation here: a parthood relation in the case of the former and a membership relation in the case of the latter. Indeed, very often grounding seems to work this way – the presence of a grounding relation is parasitic on the presence of an additional relation. This raises a number of very interesting conceptual questions around how grounding stands to the more familiar relations of parthood, membership, and so on;, and what conception of grounding we ought to be operating with. I'm not interested in even attempting to answer the second of these questions, but I will say something more about the former.

We can draw a distinction between big-G Grounding, for present purposes, GROUNDING, and small-g grounding, grounding.[12] On the big-G conception, there is a generic relation of ground distinctive from the small-g relations, and it is *this* relation that is the primary structuring relation, or at least the relation that many philosophers have in mind when they talk about grounding. On the small-g conception, what we are talking about when talking about grounding just are the small-g relations such as membership, proper parthood, the subset and the determinate/determinable relations, for example. On this approach, to say that

---

[12] See Wilson (2014) for the most widely cited discussion of these two conceptions of grounding and why we should prefer one over the other. See also Koslicki (2015) for a slightly different but very interesting discussion of related matters.

x grounds y is *always* to say that x is a part of y, or that x is a member of y, or something of the like. Regardless of which approach one prefers, both leave open the question of what exactly the relationship is between big-G and small-g grounding relations.

One possible way of understanding the relationship between GROUNDING and the grounding relations is in terms of the *genus/species* distinction. On such an approach, GROUNDING is the genus, with the small-g relations serving as its species. Parthood and membership stand to GROUNDING in the same way that wolves and domestic dogs stand to *canis*. A second approach takes GROUNDING to serve as a *covering term*. On this approach, just as when we talk about things, we are always talking about shoes, bottles, pyjamas, and so on, when we talk about GROUNDING, we are always talking about parthood, membership, the determinate/determinable connection, etc.[13] Still a third way takes GROUNDING to be a *sui generis* relation that possibly, but not necessarily, tracks what we are referring to as the small-g relations. Schaffer's account of GROUNDING seems to work in this way. As we will see in Section 4, Schaffer's preferred account of the structure of the world has grounding running in the opposite direction to the mereological composition relation.

The question of how best to understand the big-G/small-g distinction and their relationship to one another intersects in an interesting way with a second metaphysical issue. Let us suppose that we are operating with a notion of GROUNDING – on the generic conception. Suppose, also, that we are of the view that everything is either grounded or ungrounded – so grounding is exclusive and exhaustive. The employment of the notion of GROUNDING is conducive to the idea that reality has an overarching structure, that the entire contents of reality are pulled into an enormous metaphysical superstructure. A view according to which all talk of grounding just is talk in terms of the small-g relations opens up the possibility of a different understanding of how the world is arranged. On this second conception, we can allow that orderings are relativized. So, for example, some fact may appear in the mereological ordering without entering into any kind of relation at all with some other entity in the determinate/determinable ordering. On this second conception, there need not be an overarching superstructure ordered by a GROUNDING relation into which absolutely everything is pulled.

So far, I have simply referred to grounding. It is important to recognize that the distinction can be drawn between *full* and *partial* grounding. Consider again the relationship between {Socrates} and Socrates or between the fact that the

---

[13] See Thomassen (2007), chapter 11, for a discussion of the notion of a covering term.

building is sleek or modern and the fact that the building is sleek. In both cases, the grounded entity is *fully* grounded in its grounds. The existence of Socrates is sufficient to make it the case that his singleton exists, just as the fact that the building is sleek is sufficient to make it the case that the building is sleek or modern. Consider, instead, the relationship between Socrates and his liver or the relationship between the fact that the building is sleek and modern and the fact that the building is sleek. The existence of Socrates' liver is not sufficient for the existence of Socrates, nor is the fact that the building is sleek sufficient for it to be the case that the building is sleek and modern. In these cases, we say that the grounded entity is merely *partially* grounded in that which grounds it. There is much more that needs to be said about full and partial grounding, but for now, the literature on this topic is underdeveloped.

1.2 Fundamentality

We come now to consideration of the notion of fundamentality, but first, a quick detour through foundational epistemology. According to the Agrippa Trilemma, the structure of justification admits of three possibilities. In order for any inferentially justified belief to be ultimately justified, it can be a member of a chain of beliefs that terminates in a belief (or set of beliefs) that are not themselves inferentially justified – that are non-inferentially justified. This is what it is to be an *epistemic foundationalist*. Alternatively, an inferentially justified belief can be ultimately justified by being a member of an infinitely long chain of inferentially justified beliefs – a chain that never bottoms out. This is what it is to be an *epistemic infinitist*. The third remaining possibility is that inferentially justified beliefs are ultimately justified by dint of being members of chains of beliefs that bottom out in self-justifying beliefs or are members of chains that form a loop. This last kind of approach is known as *epistemic coherentism*.[14]

The Agrippa Trilemma of justification can be mirrored in the set of positions available in foundational metaphysics. Broadly speaking, then, there are three possible views as regards the overarching structure of the world. According to the *metaphysical foundationalist*, reality is hierarchically arranged, with chains of entities ordered by relations of ground ultimately grounding out in something fundamental. According to the *metaphysical infinitist*, reality is hierarchically arranged, where chains of entities ordered by relations of ground do *not* ultimately ground out in something

---

[14] There are versions of epistemic coherentism that demand more than this, namely, a web of beliefs sufficiently rich enough to generate justification. Versions of metaphysical coherentism can also be understood in this way.

fundamental. The *metaphysical coherentist* agrees with the infinitist that there is nothing fundamental, but disagrees with both the foundationalist and the infinitist about reality's overarching shape. According to the metaphysical coherentist, then, reality admits of circular structures and contains nothing fundamental.

Not everyone agrees that all three of the aforementioned views are metaphysically possible. Undeniably, though, the default setting amongst contemporary analytic metaphysicians is that metaphysical foundationalism is true. Typically understood as a package of views that most commonly involves commitment to the thought that the world is a fundamentally physical place, that what serves as the absolutely fundamental ground is itself physical, or about the physical. One need not buy the whole package – foundationalism is open to the theist, the anti-realist, the idealist, and so on – but packed into most foundationalists' commitments are a fleet of additional beliefs about what kind of broad picture of the nature of reality is correct.

This notion of *absolute fundamentality* is not the only notion of fundamentality that does work in the contemporary literature. The paperweight on the desk in front of me seems *less fundamental than* the molecules that compose it, and conversely, the molecules are *more fundamental than* the paperweight. It is reasonable to suppose that the paperweight on my desk is neither more nor less but *equally fundamental with* the paperweight on my husband's desk. These relations – the relations of more-fundamental-than, less-fundamental-than and equifundamental-with – are relations of *relative fundamentality*.[15]

There are, thus, two senses of fundamentality in operation in the contemporary literature, absolute and relative. In the rest of this Element, I shall be focused upon absolute fundamentality. Why? There are a few reasons for this. First, the thought that there is something fundamental is old. Indeed, concerns over (absolute) fundamentality have been front and centre throughout the history of the Western tradition; they have also illuminated much non-Western philosophy as well. And so much of metaphysics has been preoccupied with the particular philosophical problems that fundamental entities present us with. Second, the notion of relative fundamentality strikes me as being *conceptually* posterior to that of absolute fundamentality. The notion of relative fundamentality makes sense against a background understanding of the notion of absolute fundamentality. The metaphysics of relative fundamentality does not *require* that there *is* something fundamental – things can be more or less fundamental than other things without their needing to be anything that is absolutely

---

[15] See Bennett (2018), esp. section 5 for a developed discussion of the notion of relative fundamentality.

fundamental. But I do believe that the language of (relative) fundamentality, as it pertains to an ordering in reality, is sensical exactly because it is evocative of the idea that some things are more or less important than other things (metaphysically speaking) in relation to something absolutely basic.

1.2.1 Absolute Fundamentality

The metaphysical foundationalist is committed to the idea that there is something that is fundamental. Let us call this the *fundamentality thesis*.

Fundamentality thesis: there is some x such that x is fundamental.

Beyond the stipulation of a bald commitment to the idea that there is something fundamental, the fundamentality thesis invites a number of important and interesting questions. Can the notion of fundamentality be further analysed? Must the fundamenta be connected to the non-fundamenta? If so, how? What kinds of things are or can be fundamental? Why suppose there is anything fundamental in the first place? As we shall see, much of the rest of this Element will be devoted to thinking through how best to answer these questions. For now, however, let us begin by addressing some preliminary considerations.

Although not a common view, some philosophers believe that the notion of fundamentality is primitive – it is deserving of no further analysis. Kit Fine holds that fundamentality 'is a primitive metaphysical concept ... that cannot be understood in fundamentally different terms', and Jessica Wilson has argued that 'the fundamental is, well, fundamental'.[16] These important outliers aside, we can find four analyses of fundamentality in the literature.

1.2.1.1 Independence

It is by now quite standard for philosophers to analyse fundamentality in terms of grounding. In particular, it is standard to think that the best definition of fundamentality is as follows:[17]

Fundamental$_{INDEPENDENT}$: $\forall x$, x is fundamental if x is ungrounded.

This grounding-based definition of fundamentality not only allows us to understand what fundamentality consists in but also captures an important aspect of fundamentality: *independence*. As will become particularly salient in Section 2, that whatever is fundamental is *in some important sense* independent is a core, if

---

[16] Fine (2001), p. 1, and Wilson (2014), p. 560.

[17] Jessica Wilson (2014) is perhaps the best-known discussion by someone who denies the need and value of further analysing fundamentality in any other terms.

not the core, feature of fundamentality as it has been historically conceived. It is also the core feature of most accounts of fundamentality contemporarily.

As detailed in section 1.1.3, there are two different conceptions of grounding – GROUNDING versus small-g. Depending on how we are to understand these two conceptions, different ways of understanding Fundamental$_{\text{INDEPENDENCE}}$ will be open to us:

(1) x is Fundamental$_{\text{INDEPENDENT}}$: $\forall R_G \sim \exists y\, R_G yx$
(2) x is Fundamental$_{\text{INDEPENDENT}}$: $\forall R_g \sim \exists y R_g yx$
(3) x is Fundamental$_{\text{INDEPENDENT}}$: $\exists R_g \sim \exists y R_g yx$

It can first be noted that (1)–(3) do not demand independence *tout court*. It may be the case that x is Fundamental$_{\text{INDEPENDENT}}$ and, yet, causally dependent, for example.[18] Wielding a big-G notion of grounding, R_G, a commitment to independence is understood as entailing that if x is fundamental then there is nothing to which x stands in the relation R_G, as per (1). Wielding, on the other hand, small-g relations, it is open that for some x, that x not stand in any small-g relation, R_g, whatsoever to any y, as per (2), or that x not stand in some particular small-g relation, R_g, to any y, as per (3). In this latter case, it remains possible that although x is fundamental relative to some particular small-g ordering, it is *not* fundamental relative to some other.

1.2.1.2 Completeness

A second available conception of fundamentality is in terms of what Karen Bennett labels *completeness*.[19] The idea, however, is old. In creating the world, that which is fundamental is *all that God needed to create*. It is from the fundamental that all else is derived; and it is in its terms that everything else can be explained. In being complete, the fundamental level gives rise to and allows us to account for everything else – all the non-fundamental stuff. We can capture this sense of fundamentality as follows:

Fundamental$_{\text{COMPLETEe}}$: the xxs or some x is complete if and only if the xxs or x at world w ground(s) everything else at w.

Generally, though, there is more packed into this notion of completeness than the simple idea that the fundamental allows us to account for everything else. In

---

[18] This will depend partly on how we think about causation and its relation to grounding. But even if we think that causing is a kind of grounding (or vice versa), it is still the case that Fundamental$_{\text{INDEPENDENT}}$ does not entail independence *tout court* as it leaves open the possibility that something that is Fundamental$_{\text{INDEPENDENT}}$ bears some other kind of non-grounding relation to something else.
[19] Bennett (2018), p. 107.

particular, when wielding this sense of fundamentality, philosophers tend to have in mind a consideration of parsimony. Not only does God only need to create the fundamental – so, say, all the particles – but God only needs to create the exact or minimal number of particles required to give us everything else. What this leaves us with is an understanding of fundamentality according to which the fundamental provides a *unique minimally complete* basis for everything else.

> Fundamental$_{\text{UMCOMPLETE}}$: the *xx*s or some *x* is uniquely minimally complete if and only if the *xx*s or *x* at world *w* ground everything else at *w*, where no subset (or subplurality) or *xx*s is complete and there is no other *xx*s or *x* that is complete.

1.2.1.3 Indispensability

Raven (2016) draws a distinction between two theses:

FUNDAMENTALISM: Necessarily, something is fundamental.

FOUNDATIONALISM: Necessarily, something is fundamental if and only if it is foundational.

The two of which lead to a puzzle when combined with a third thesis:

ABYSSALISM: Possibly, nothing is foundational.[20]

In order to resolve this puzzle, Raven argues against FOUNDATIONALISM by denying that the only way to be fundamental is to be foundational. In particular, he argues for the possibility of fundamentality *without* foundations by arguing for an account of fundamentality understood, instead, in terms of *ineliminability*. Informally, imagine that the world is gunky – there are no partless parts. Suppose that the fact that some whole, *M*, is material and that its materiality is grounded in the materiality of its parts. So, the fact that *M* is material is grounded in the fact that its right and left parts are material. But these further facts – the fact that the right part is material and the fact that the left part is material – are themselves grounded in further facts about the materiality of their parts. As the world is gunky, the divisibility of these parts extends on *ad infinitum*. Note, though, that the property *being material* appears at every stage of the grounding chain – even at infinity, as it were, it will still be there. For Raven, then, this property – *being material* – is *ineliminable* and, thus, fundamental (without being foundational). The property never disappears or is grounded away, for want of a better expression. Nothing is foundational on this

---

[20] Raven (2017), p. 608.

picture; there is nothing that exists independently and terminates our grounding chain. There is, however, something fundamental, namely, the property *being material*. Broadly construed, according to this approach, 'the fundamental is discovered by examining the topology of which facts ground which and discerning which entities within the topology are ineliminable'.[21]

1.2.1.4 Naturalness

The two figures cited most often as proponents of understanding fundamentality in terms of naturalness are David Lewis and, following him, Ted Sider. According to Lewis, 'fundamental properties are those properties that I have elsewhere called "perfectly natural"', and 'physics has its short list of "fundamental physical properties" . . . what physics has undertaken, . . . is an inventory of the sparse properties . . . when a property [is sparse], I call it a natural property'.[22] For Sider, extending the Lewisian notion of naturalness to yield his notion of structure, he 'connect[s] structure to fundamentality. The joint-carving notions are the fundamental notions; a fact is fundamental when it is stated in joint-carving terms'.[23] He believes that 'a central task of metaphysics has always been to discern the ultimate or fundamental reality underlying the appearances', and that he 'think[s] of this task as the investigation of reality's structure'.[24]

What are perfectly natural properties and structure? For Lewis, natural properties capture facts of resemblance, causal powers, they carve reality at its joints, they are intrinsic, sparse – 'there are only just enough of them to characterize things completely and without redundancy'[25]– they distinguish the laws of nature from other Humean generalizations, they are 'reference magnets' and they help characterize duplicates. As naturalness comes in degrees, it is the perfectly natural properties that would be the fundamental ones. For Sider, as already stated, structure is linked to joint-carving as well. He extends talk of joint-carvers beyond properties and predicates to include expressions of any grammatical category. For Sider, then, we can ask of logical connectives such as 'and' and 'or' whether they are joint-carving and thus natural and fundamental.

Neither Lewis nor Sider connects their notions of naturalness to those of independence or grounding. In fact, Sider is explicit that conceptions of fundamentality framed in terms of grounding are rival views.[26] It is also the case that it is not hard to come up with examples of entities that would appear to be natural and *not* independent. Consider, for example, sets (properties just are sets for Lewis). Sets are perfectly natural for Lewis and yet clearly not

---

[21] Raven (2017), p. 623.   [22] Lewis (2009), p. 204, and Lewis (1986), p. 60.
[23] Sider (2011), vii.   [24] Sider (2011).   [25] Lewis (1986), 60.   [26] Sider (2011), chapter 8

independently existent, for they are constructed out of, and dependent upon, their members.

1.3 Unexplained . . .

It is an interesting question what the conceptual connections are between our different conceptions of fundamentality. It is also important to understand what our, *the*, central conception of fundamentality is. There is much that could be said here, but I shall cut to the heart of it.

I will be leaving behind both Indispensability and Naturalness. In the case of Indispensability, I leave it behind because it strikes me as an (possibly perfectly legitimate) *alternative* to foundationalism without being an obvious replacement for it. I leave behind Naturalness because it seems needlessly ontologically loaded; this is because on some views, at least, it demands understanding fundamentality in terms of properties. More broadly, foundationalism understood in terms of perfect naturalness looks to be a framework ill equipped to accommodate the likes of God or the cosmos as contenders for fundamental entities. Finally, neither Indispensability nor Naturalness comports with notions of fundamentality as they have been understood broadly – historically and across traditions.

The central conception of fundamentality is that of Fundamental$_{\text{INDEPENDENT}}$. Something is fundamental if and only if it is independent, which is just to say that something is fundamental if and only if it is ungrounded. As seen in section 1.2.1.1, this commitment can express itself in different ways – (1)–(3) – depending on whether we are operating with a big-G or a small-g conception of grounding. Two of these ways deliver what we might think of as a notion of *absolute* absolute fundamentality – (1) and (2) – versus the third way, (3), which yields a kind of *relativized* absolute fundamentality.

In case this distinction seems like a useless one, consider the difference between taking, say, God, as what is fundamental versus, say, atomic facts. In the case of God, God is absolutely unequivocally – absolutely absolutely – fundamental. There is nothing that God is grounded in, and nothing that things other than God are ultimately grounded upon that isn't God. Contrast this with the case of atomic facts. Although, say, conjunctive facts may ultimately depend upon atomic facts – facts that are not grounded in further facts – atomic facts need not be the absolute rock bottom of every ordering. A constituent of an atomic fact may well have parts where those parts ground out in a simple substance, for example. On such a view, there are at least two kinds of fundamental entities, atomic facts and simple substances, which serve as the terminus points for different, relativized grounding orderings. Moving forward, though, much of what I say will hold equally well for whichever conception of fundamentality one chooses to work with. If anything hangs on drawing a distinction between absolute absolute fundamentality and relativized absolute fundamentality, I will draw the reader's attention to it.

All Fundamental$_{INDEPENDENCE}$ tells us is that something is fundamental just in case it is ungrounded. On a picture of reality according to which there are three atoms, these three atoms all count as fundamental. Alternatively, imagine an account on which a is grounded in b, which is ungrounded, and there is also one atom, c. On such a picture, b and c are both fundamental, and a is the only dependent entity. Fundamental$_{INDEPENDENCE}$ demands nothing as regards how fundamental entities are connected to anything else. This leaves open the possibility that there are fundamental entities that bear no explanatory connections to anything else, which is tantamount to saying that Fundamental$_{INDEPENDENCE}$ leaves it open that there are fundamental entities that don't do any explanatory work (as in the case of c).

Many philosophers seem happy to accept this configuration of commitments. At least they seem happy to take Fundamental$_{INDEPENDENCE}$ as the *definition* of fundamentality, introducing something like Fundamental$_{UMCOMPLETENESS}$ as a desideratum on the notion. Can more be said about the relationship between Fundamental$_{INDEPENDENCE}$ and Fundamental$_{UMCOMPLETENESS}$, though? Employing set-theoretic considerations, Karen Bennett argues that there is a uniquely minimal set, the set which contains all, and only, the independent entities. Her argumentation is dense and I will not rehearse it here. For Bennett, then, although Fundamental$_{INDEPENDENCE}$ and Fundamental$_{UMCOMPLETENESS}$ are conceptually distinct, there are tight and important connections between them; so much so that the only entities that make it into 'all that God needed to create', or the 'blueprint for reality', just are the independent entities.[27]

Bennett's set-theoretic arguments aside, are there other ways in which we might understand connections between the two principles? There are. One such connection is particularly important and will form the subject matter of much of the next section, to which we now turn.

2 Ultimate Explanations: An Idea and Its History

In much of the literature that is directly about – as well as the literature that makes reference to – fundamentality, one can also find reference to ultimacy. The contemporary literature on grounding and fundamentality is shot through with talk of how things are, or what there must be, ultimately.

---

[27] Bennett (2017), ch. 5.6.

This is interesting for a number of reasons. First, it connects talk of grounding and fundamentality to concepts with which we are already familiar. One can find reference to ultimate explainers, ultimate explanations and talk of how things ultimately are right the way through the philosophical literature more broadly. This connection to something outside itself – outside the concepts of grounding and fundamentality – can help us to get purchase on what grounding folks are on about and what kind of business talk of fundamentality is in. Second to this, the appeal to ultimacy in discussions of grounding and fundamentality places the contemporary grounding literature in a continuum with a very old and venerable literature: a literature associated with God, The One, Being, Ultimate Reality and atomisms, for example. Understanding this connection should also help fortify our understanding of contemporary talk of fundamentality, as well as illuminate just what is at stake.

Before moving into a discussion of ultimate explainers as metaphysical posits and ultimate explanations, I would first like to address an issue that will no doubt already be ringing in certain kinds of heads: but aren't the notions of grounding and fundamentality recent inventions?

2.1 Grounding Old or New?

Anyone familiar with the contemporary grounding literature will be aware that there is something of a tension or, perhaps better to say, divergence of opinion over the history of the notion. On one view, the notion of grounding is thought to be as old as philosophy itself, with many of its most important thinkers engaging with questions pertaining to it. On this approach, although more contemporary discussions certainly take on their own flavour, the resurgence in interest in the notion is very much entangled with a return to the glorious days of good old-fashioned metaphysics. On another view, the notion of grounding is very much the plaything of contemporary analytic metaphysicians. According to this understanding of grounding, its origin myth traces itself back to Manhattan in the early noughties, where Kit Fine, Gideon Rosen and Jonathan Schaffer laid the foundations for a new and important program of research. *Mutatis mutandis* for the notion of fundamentality assuming it to be married to and/or defined in terms of grounding.

How is it that such seemingly juxtaposed views of the history of grounding have come to characterise the discourse? Which one is correct? These are difficult (and partly, if not largely, sociological) questions and I won't really attempt to answer them here. What I will do, however, is try to say something more about how we might *characterize* these different conceptions of grounding and its relationship to history, as well as to defend the position that will illuminate the rest of this Element: the notions of grounding and fundamentality can reasonably be understood as old, if not in letter, then at least in spirit.

Michael Raven suggests that one good way of accounting for divergent views on the history of grounding is in terms of a distinction between *questions of ground* and *questions about ground*.[28] When Socrates asks in the *Euthyphro* if someone is pious because he is loved by the gods, or if he is loved by the gods because he is pious, Plato is directing our attention to a *question of ground*. When, in the contemporary literature, philosophers are debating whether grounding is necessarily asymmetric, transitive and irreflexive, they are asking *questions about ground*. The divergent views about the history of grounding, then, can be better understood in terms of a divergence in the kinds of grounding questions philosophers are, and have been, interested in. Historically, so the thinking might go, philosophers have been interested in questions *of* grounding, whereas the contemporary literature has been primarily focused on questions *about* ground. The notion of grounding is as old as the hills, with the more recent focus in the literature simply being directed at the notion itself.

Although this characterization is appealing, it surely has its limitations. Let us grant for the moment that it is correct to say that historically, philosophers have been concerned with questions of ground – as we will see, even this claim is contentious. It would also seem undeniable that contemporary discussions have been heavy on questions about the nature of grounding: is it best expressed by a predicate or a sentential operator? It is important to recognize, though, that both contemporarily and historically, philosophers have been interested in both. The historical literature is by no means short of attempts at engaging with questions about ground, nor is the contemporary literature shy on questions of ground.

Perhaps a finer-grained way of understanding the difference between grounding-as-new and grounding-as-old is in terms of a distinction between questions of and about ground that are addressed *directly* or *indirectly*. Consider versions of cosmological arguments. Let us suppose that there is the totality of contingent entities, the cosmos, that needs an explanation, and that the only entity apt to explain that totality is the particular necessary being that is God. Some versions of cosmological arguments, then, look very much to be in the business of *directly* engaging *questions of ground*. Central to such arguments, though, is a crucial assumption that stipulates that no contingent entity can explain the totality of contingent entities. Debate has raged for centuries over how, exactly, we ought to understand this assumption, and whether or not we ought to believe it – with disagreements over the right way to cash out this assumption leading to

---

[28] Raven (2020).

overhauls of versions of the argument. Importantly, this assumption is generally understood as a *no-circularity* assumption – an assumption that demands consideration of the nature of the grounding relation. In debating whether or not any contingent thing can explain the existence of the cosmos, philosophers are, albeit *indirectly*, debating whether or not grounding can be reflexive. Similarly, with the very sophisticated and very old discussions around God's nature as a self-explainer. The history of philosophy is rich in discussions *about* grounding, only those discussions very often take place indirectly.

Similarly, much contemporary discussion of grounding is directly engaged with questions about grounding but also indirectly engaged with questions of grounding as well. The kinds of formal properties we take grounding to have, what we think the relata of the relations are, will have consequences for substantive metaphysical theses.[29] If we suppose that sets are grounded in their members, and that grounding is irreflexive, then non–well-founded set theories are ruled out out of the gate. Indeed, it is with certain substantive background metaphysical commitments in mind regarding what grounds what that philosophers make decisions about which formal properties they are willing to tolerate. In directly discussing questions about ground, philosophers are very often engaged, indirectly, in questions of ground as well.

So far, at best, I have defended the thought that we can reconcile the grounding-as-new view with the grounding-as-old view, and we can do this by acknowledging that contemporary and historical proponents of the notion have pressed it into service in different ways. What I haven't done, though, is given the reader any reason to believe that grounding, and, with it, fundamentality, are historically utilized notions in the first place. In order to address this point, let us begin by considering some reasons for thinking that the notion of grounding has *not* been employed by historical figures.

One reason for denying that historical figures have made use of a notion of ground is that in most of the alleged cases in which ground is the relation that seems to be at issue, the relata of those relations are *things* rather than *facts*. As many contemporary accounts of ground hold that grounding involves or obtains between propositions or facts, such historic cases cannot be ones in which the notion of grounding is at work after all. Typically, when we talk about everything depending on God, we mean that *things* depend on God as a *thing*, and not that the fact that I exist is grounded in the fact that God exists, for example. Second to this, very often in the historic literature the language of grounding is not deployed. What is deployed is language that picks out concepts that we think

---

[29] I have in mind here debates over the possibility of non–well-founded set theories and mereologies, for example.

of as *not* being those of grounding. Consider much of the discussion around the Principle of Sufficient Reason (PSR). There we see talk of *causes* and *reasons*, but not historically of grounding. If causing is not grounding but sufficient reasons are causes, then the PSR is not a principle tied up with the notion of grounding. Finally, very often the relation involved in historic accounts that might seem like providing example cases of grounding just exhibits the wrong features. According to Leibniz (2017a), God is self-causing or self-explanatory. Leibniz does not mean that God flings Himself into existence, but rather that God's existence can be accounted for internally to God (it is part of God's essence that He exist). But if God's existence is self-explanatory, it cannot be because it is self-grounded in the sense in which contemporary thinkers understand it. This is tantamount to saying that there is at least one instance of the grounding relation that is reflexive; and as grounding is asymmetric, whatever relation Leibniz is employing, it cannot be grounding.[30]

Although philosophers have expressed doubts over the extended history of the notion of grounding, many more have defended the thought that it is of historic significance. In Aristotle, the case can be made that his notions of material and formal causes are notions of ground, as is that of demonstration in the *Posterior Analytics*.[31] In Avicenna, we find discussion of the relationship between definitions, essences and necessity that makes use of, and reflects, a conception of ground, albeit one that is interestingly different to that with which we are contemporarily familiar.[32] Abelard, inheriting from Aristotle and Boethius relations of metaphysical dependence and logical dependence respectively – both of which, it has been argued, can be understood in terms of ground – argues for the reduction of the latter to the former.[33] A thicket of issues around natural priority occupied very many of the Medievals – Aquinas, Henry of Ghent and Scotus, for example. William of Ockham was precipitous of important advances in the kinds of accounts of natural priority that worked and those that didn't – foreshadowing contemporary discussions by, in particular, Kit Fine.[34] He also made novel contributions to an understanding of the Euthyphro Dilemma in terms of something very much like a notion of normative grounding.[35] Other of the Medievals, such as Buridan, made important

---

[30] For further reading on examples of why certain important historic accounts might not be best interpreted in the language of grounding, see, for example, Amijee (2020) on grounding in Spinoza and Leibniz's accounts of the PSR. See Casati (2018) for a discussion of the thought that grounding might not be the relation that links beings to Being in Heidegger. See Corkum (2020) for a discussion that makes it clear that it is no straightforward matter to attribute a notion of ground to Aristotle.

[31] See Corkum (2020) and Malink (2020).   [32] See Thom (forthcoming).

[33] See Martin (forthcoming).   [34] See Paasch (forthcoming).   [35] See Ward (forthcoming).

contributions to shifts in our understanding of logical consequence that, again, can be thought of as properly involving notions of ground.[36]

Moving into the early modern period, there is no short supply of thinkers who appear to be operating with a notion of ground.[37] One reason for this is owing to the prominence of the PSR, which we have good reasons to believe *can* be understood in terms of grounding. Spinoza and Leibniz, for example, believed that God was the *sufficient reason* – without being the first cause – for the existence of the cosmos and, thus, its ultimate ground. At the absolute tail end of the early modern period, or the beginning of the modern period, depending on how one reckons, perhaps the most developed and sustained discussion of the notion of ground prior to the contemporary literature was offered by Bernard Bolzano.[38] What is striking about Bolzano's contribution is, drawing on an earlier distinction, how occupied he was with questions *about* grounding rather than *of* grounding. Well into the modern period, philosophers such as Heidegger and Husserl also appeared to be working with notions of ground.[39]

I have provided reasons to think that the notion of *ground* has an extended, indeed illustrious, history, but what about that of fundamentality? One immediate reason to think that the notion of fundamentality is also old is owing to its intimate association with the notion of grounding. It is the relation of ground that has, historically, very often been pressed into the service of establishing that there is something fundamental. If grounding is old, and fundamentality is defined in terms of grounding, the notion of fundamentality is old as well. Consider the Leibnizian version of the cosmological argument. Although there needs not be a first *cause*, there does need to be an ultimate ground – God – that serves as the sufficient reason (ground) for the contingent things. It is because things have sufficient reasons (grounds) that God (*qua* fundamentum) must exist.

That the notion of fundamentality can be connected to that of grounding, and that grounding is old, is not, however, the only – nor, perhaps, the most compelling – reason to think that the notion of fundamentality is old as well. A further reason for thinking that fundamentality is old is that contemporary thinkers often employ language evocative of that as historically associated with certain kinds of philosophical projects. Just as contemporary thinkers talk about reality as needing an *ultimate ground* or things being thus and such a way *ultimately*, many historic figures have spoken in exactly these same terms. Perhaps most compellingly, though, the reason to think that the notion of

---

[36] See C. Normore, (forthcoming).
[37] See, for example, Della Rocca (2010) and Amijee (2020).   [38] See Roski (2020).
[39] Casati (2018, 2021) and Mulligan (2020).

fundamentality is old is that it is so conceptually similar to notions that we can find right the way through the history of philosophy. Much of what remains of this section will be devoted to fleshing out this particular idea.

2.2 Ultimate Explanations

The notion of ultimacy is not only old, but seemingly universal. The history of Western philosophy is littered with accounts that posit various kinds of entities invoked in service to the idea that something or other needs an ultimate explanation. In the Eastern traditions, on the other hand, Brahman, the Dao and Emptiness, for example, are all candidate examples of ultimate posits. Posits that, like their Western counterparts, are invoked in service to very particular explanatory ends.

Timothy O'Connor defines an ultimate explanation as 'a natural or nonarbitrary stopping point (even if only a schematic one) to the nested series of available plausible explanations for increasingly general aspects of the world'.[40] The most general aspect of the world is the fact that anything exists whatsoever. Perhaps the paradigmatic example of an ultimate explanation, then, can be found in the form of God whose existence is arrived at by way of a cosmological argument. These arguments start by isolating something that stands in need of explanation – the fact that anything exists whatsoever, or that there is something rather than nothing, or something of the like – and, in combination with several assumptions, arrive at the conclusion that God must exist. God ultimately explains the contents of the cosmos.

But ultimate explanations need not only target the *most general* aspect of the world. There are general, but not the most general, aspects of the world that also stand in need of explanation. Consider, for example, what is at issue in foundational epistemology – the structure and nature of justified belief. In particular, what foundational epistemologists are concerned with is establishing how it is that beliefs are arranged such that we come to have *any* justified beliefs in the first place. The worry is not how we are justified in thinking that today is Sunday or that the sun is hot, but how any belief is justified whatsoever. In positing noninferentially justified, basic beliefs, the epistemic foundationalist is offering an ultimate explanation of how a general aspect of reality – belief – is possible. The epistemic infinitist, on the other hand, holds that the ultimate explanation of belief requires no such basic entities.

Although the aforementioned explanatory projects vary in their scope, we can see how they share in certain kinds of patterns. First, ultimate explanations begin by asking a question about the existence or obtaining of something in its

---

generality: why is there anything whatsoever? How are there any justified beliefs? These questions are then reformulated to give us an *explanatory target* that is used as a premise in argument that delivers as its conclusion an ultimate explainer. [] stands in for 'the fact that . . .'

Explanatory Target: [x is] or x stands in need of explanation

Second, ultimate explanations involve assumptions about how things need to be or how things can't be such that the explanatory target can be satisfied. These assumptions deliver the result that we have reasons to believe that certain kinds of things are *not apt* to explain our target, resulting, eventually, in an argument that tells us what is. In the case of versions of cosmological arguments, for example, they contain assumptions, the upshot of which are that no contingent thing can explain why there are any contingent things whatsoever. These assumptions generally involve appeal to a problem of circularity (even if not explicitly stated) and, importantly, force us beyond the collection of things to be explained. I shall call them *externality assumptions* – which can be many and often involve sub-arguments. We can put them schematically as follows:

Externality Assumptions: [x is f] or x cannot explain [x is F] or x.

To help illustrate the broad idea here, let us consider more fully now a version of a cosmological argument. Cosmological arguments begin by making some fairly unremarkable assumptions about the existence and nature of the world and move from there to the existence of God. Here is a sketch of just such an argument:

(1) There is a totality of all contingent things, *C*.
(2) The totality of all contingent things stands in need of explanation.
(3) No contingent thing can explain the totality of contingent things.
    (a) If x is contingent, then x is a member of *C*.
    (b) If x explains *C*, then *C* is explained in terms of itself.
    (c) Nothing can be self-explanatory.
(4) Everything is either contingent or necessary but not both.
(5) Therefore, what explains *C* must be necessary.
(6) The necessary being that explains *C* is God.

In this version of the argument, line 2 looks to state our explanatory target. The assumption at line 3, and its sub-argument, deliver our externality assumptions. It is here that we are provided with reasons to believe that whatever explains the cosmos cannot be contingent – we are pushed beyond the collection of contingent things to something necessary. Obviously, the move from line 5 to line 6 requires additional assumptions, but as they are not relevant to the discussion here, I leave them out.

Ultimate explanations are explanations that aim at explaining some phenomenon in its generality. An ultimate explanation aims at answering questions such as 'why is there anything whatsoever?', 'how are there justified beliefs?' and so on. The answer to these sorts of questions is never meant to be 'because Kevin exists' or 'because I am justified in thinking Kevin exists'. At least ultimate explanations are not typically thought of in this way. Ultimate explanations are derived by way of an argument that stipulates an explanatory target and contains several assumptions that move us to an ultimate explainer. I shall come back to a discussion of how these arguments work, but for now let us move on to what these explanations deliver: ultimate explainers.

2.3 Ultimate Explainers

Ultimate explainers are the posits of ultimate explanations that do the relevant explanatory work. But what criteria must these posits meet in order to be considered adequate to the task? Let us look at O'Connor's definition again:

ULTIMATE EXPLANATION$_{def}$: a natural or non-arbitrary stopping point (even if only a schematic one) to the nested series of available plausible explanations for increasingly general aspects of the world.

Assuming as per above that ultimate explainers are the posits of ultimate explanations that perform the relevant explanatory work, the first point of note is that our ultimate explainers should provide a *natural* or *non-arbitrary* stopping point. The second point of note is that they should be *explanatory*. The third point of note is that they should be *plausibly* relevant to the task at hand. Let us consider each desideratum in its turn.

What does it mean for an explanatory stopping point to be natural or non-arbitrary? Presumably, here, the naturalness at issue is not naturalness as understood in terms of suitability, lest the second, plausibility constraint, be rendered superfluous. Nor is the naturalness to be understood in the sense of, say, Lewisian natural properties. A better way of understanding the relevant notions of naturalness or non-arbitrariness is in terms of the thought that the explainer, itself, is not beholden to the same explanatory demands that lead to our positing it in the first place. In other words, some *explanandum* is natural or non-arbitrary insofar as we are *not compelled to go beyond it – it does not stand in need of explanation*.

What does it mean for a natural or non-arbitrary stopping point to be explanatory? It seems reasonable to suppose that for a natural stopping point to be explanatory it needs to be connected to what it is supposed to be explaining in the right kind of way. If causes explain, then a causal connection between A and B looks like the right kind of connection to allow A to explain B. If the connection between grounding and explaining is as most folks say, then because grounds explain, grounding also looks like the right kind of connection to have between A and B, such that A might explain B.

What does it mean for a non-arbitrary explanatory stopping point to be plausible? Intuitively, the flying spaghetti monster doesn't seem like a plausible ultimate explainer for the existence of the cosmos (or even just for the existence of spaghetti). What counts as a plausible non-arbitrary stopping point in an explanatory chain will be fixed (partly) by the background theoretical framework in which the explanations are generated. Operating in a naturalistic framework, whatever serve as ultimate explainers will be part of the natural world. Against a background of Christian theological commitments, God will serve as a plausible non-arbitrary stopping point to certain kinds of explanatory chains. Internal to a given framework, the plausibility of explanations will be fixed by the explanatory relations. In the case of causal connections, for example, as numbers aren't causally efficacious, numbers won't be plausible causal explainers. In the case of grounding relations, those relations will help delineate what our plausible explainers are.

That said, I actually think there are some very interesting philosophical issues raised here. Thinking again about grounding, we generally take it for granted that it's obvious or intuitive what grounds what. Our theorizing about grounding typically *starts* by taking widely agreed upon example instances of grounding and generalizing from there. But beyond what we think of as data in the case of grounding, not much, if anything at all, has been said about what kind of criteria something must meet in order to plausibly ground something else. Broader framework level considerations will help us narrow down the kinds of things that are apt to serve as grounds of other things, but internal to those frameworks, it is not at all easy to say what criterion must hold in order for something to plausibly ground something else.

Returning to our definitions of absolute fundamentality from Section 1, we can now reflect on how they intersect with the notion of an ultimate explanation. If some x is independently existent, then that x is possibly apt to serve as an ultimate explainer as that x possibly provides a natural or non-arbitrary stopping point to the nested series of available plausible explanations for increasingly general aspects of the world. And it provides a natural stopping point in virtue of its independence – exactly what such entities do not stand in need of is further explanation. Fundamental$_{\text{INDEPENDENCE}}$ captures an important aspect of the demands placed on an ultimate explanation. Note, however, that whilst the independence criterion might provide a necessary condition on something's serving as an ultimate explainer, it cannot provide a sufficient condition. Why? That something is independent is not enough to secure its role as an *explainer*, let alone a *plausible* explainer.[41] In order to secure some x's status as an ultimate explainer it needs not only to be independent, but also connected to whatever it is explaining in the right kind of way. In our case, that right kind of way is going to be by way of the grounding relation.

What of the plausibility constraint? One might suppose that this constraint is met simply by establishing what grounds what. Sets are grounded in their members and by virtue of being so grounded, those grounds can be considered plausible. The existence of my singleton set is grounded in the existence of me and not my dog's left front paw because decisions about what grounds what are made in a setting in which we have *already determined* what plausibly serves as a ground and what doesn't. By the time we are buying into a theory of grounding, we are buying into a picture of reality on which what count as plausible explainers has already been determined. Members get to ground their sets because they have already passed the plausibility test. It is highly implausible that the set-theoretic universe is grounded in the state of Texas.

Pulling these threads together, Fundamental$_{\text{INDEPENDENCE}}$ alone isn't rich enough to deliver ultimate explainers. It delivers, at best, a necessary condition on something's counting as an ultimate explainer without being sufficient. Nothing can be an ultimate explainer if it's not an explainer in the first place. Put differently, typically, we think of the posits of an ultimate explanation as *unexplained explainers*. What Fundamental$_{\text{INDEPENDENCE}}$ delivers is one face of this, something unexplained, without getting us all the way to what the project – engaging in ultimate explanations – demands. Fundamental$_{\text{UMCOMPLETENESS}}$ or some modified version of it relativized to a restricted domain, on the other hand, ensures that whatever is fundamental grounds everything else (or some subset of it). If we wish to understand fundamentality in terms of ultimate explanations – which, I shall go on to argue, we ought to – then our definition of fundamentality needs to capture *both* that our fundamenta are independent and that they ground everything else. I propose, then, that we work with the following definition:

Fundamental$_{\text{ULTIMATE}}$: for all x, x is fundamental if x is independent and x is amongst the xxs at world w that ground everything else at world w.

---

[41] Where something's being independently existent is sufficient for it to be considered fundamental (ultimate), we allow the possibility of 'fundamental' entities that are not connected to anything else in the right kind of way. We could have an island universe in which all the non-fundamental things are in relations of ground to each other, but all the 'fundamental' things are in a separate island universe and, thus, not connected to anything else.

2.4 Some Historic Examples

Armed as we are with a better understanding of ultimate explanations and the explainers that they posit, let us look, now, to some historically noteworthy examples of such explanations.

2.4.1 Prime Matter

In order to account for substance and change – and how substances can undergo change, in particular – Aristotle of the *Metaphysics* posits the existence of prime matter. Substances for Aristotle are things like people, flamingos and piano keys; they are picked out by the subjects of sentences. Substances have properties – such as being old, pink or fashioned from ivory. These properties are picked out by predicates. Consistent with Aristotle's hylomorphism, substances are fusions of form and matter. I, for example, have the form of *personhood* and that form is instantiated in my matter. Substances undergo change. And there are two sorts of change that we should be careful to distinguish. The first kind of change is *alteration*. If I leave the house to go for a walk, I lose the property of *being at home* and am, thus, altered. The second kind of change is *coming to be* or *ceasing to be* – this is the kind of change that a substance undergoes when it comes into or goes out of existence. When I die, I will undergo this kind of change. With this second kind of change, the change is characterized by the loss of form (and replacement with a different form). So, when I perish, the form of *personhood* loses its relationship to my matter and that matter comes to instantiate a new form – *corpsehood*, perhaps.

Something interesting happens to substances here, though. I die, the substance that was me has gone out of existence, but the matter that constituted me remains and takes on a new form, giving us a new substance, my corpse. Let us suppose that my matter has an additional form as well, *fleshhood*. The matter that constitutes me, after all, also seems to have its own particular forms; it's not just brute matter. As far as my flesh is concerned, though, its relationship to the properties of *personhood* and *corpsehood* is accidental. Flesh that is animated by a soul, as it were, doesn't cease to be flesh when that soul departs and only a corpse remains. What we can see, then, is that substances and their possibility for change exhibit a kind of hierarchical structure. Matter at level 3, L_3, is a substance at level 2, L_2. Change occurs when matter at L_3 loses its form, and that same form is an accidental property of a substance at L_2.

	Form	**Matter**		**Substance**	**Accidents**
L4	Personhood	+	Flesh	→ Me	*Australianhood*
L3	Fleshhood	+	Cells	→ Flesh	*Personhood*
L2	Cellhood	+	Molecules	→ Biological matter	*Fleshhood*
L1	Biological matterhood	+		Prime matter	

So far so good. The story doesn't end here, though. What needs to be added to this chart is a level 0, L_0, as follows:

L0   −   +   −   → Prime matter *Biological matterhood*[42]

How does Aristotle end up in this situation? First, it needs to be said that prime matter is the ultimate subject. The prime matter that constitutes me is the bearer of all of the properties possessed by all the substances that compose me. That said, prime matter itself has no form. It can't because if it did, it wouldn't be ground zero, as it were. If it had a form, that form would need to be an accident of some matter at the level below. Where Aristotle finds himself is in a situation in which, as we shall see, many great thinkers find themselves when it comes to offering ultimate explanations. In order to be up to the task – the task of accounting for substances and their capacity for change – Aristotle needs to arrive at something that is not beholden to the very explanatory principles that arrived him at such a stopping place in the first place – a stopping place that doesn't demand that we press on.

Unfortunately, Aristotle is not particularly forthcoming about why it is that we need prime matter. One reasonable assumption is that given Aristotle's opposition to infinities, it is hardly a surprise that he felt the need to terminate the downward sequence. There is a sense, though, in which it doesn't really matter for our purposes why or whether Aristotle thought that there had to be prime matter. It is enough for us to understand how Aristotle thought it behaved: and it behaves exactly as one would expect a kind of ultimate explainer to. On the one hand, prime matter is the ultimate ground of the possibility of substances and, on the other hand, in order to be such a ground, there cannot be anything beneath it.

---

[42] Priest (2002), chapters 5 and 6.

2.4.2 God

According to Leibniz, God is not the first cause of the cosmos, but is its sufficient reason. God, for Leibniz, exists independently of everything else and is the ultimate ground of the totality of contingent things. God looks out upon the monads – full and complete ideas of things – and chooses which of those monads to actualize. In so doing, God serves as the sufficient reason or ultimate ground of this, the actual and best, of all possible worlds.

How does Leibniz arrive at the conclusion that God is the ultimate ground rather than the first cause of things? Following Aquinas, Leibniz accepts that causal series can extend backwards in time *ad infinitum*. If A is caused by B and B by C and so on *ad infinitum*, then each effect in the sequence has its cause and can, thus, be accounted for. Although the cosmos requires no first cause in order to account for its existence, Leibniz argues that it nonetheless requires the existence of a sufficient reason:

> 'We can't find in any individual thing, or even in the entire series of things, a sufficient reason why they exist. Suppose that book on the elements of geometry has always existed, each copy made from an earlier one, with no first copy. We can explain any given copy of the book in terms of the previous book from which it was copied; but this will never lead us to a complete explanation, no matter how far back we go in the series of books. For we can always ask:
>
> Why have there always been such books?
> Why were these books written?
> Why were they written in the way they were?
>
> The different states of the world are like that series of books: each state is in a way *copied* from the preceding state ... And so with the world as with books, however far back we might go into earlier and earlier states we'll never find in *them* a complete explanation for *why there is any world at all, and *why the world is as it is.[43]

Nowhere in the world of contingent things can we find a complete explanation for the fact that there is any world at all or the fact that the world is as it is. In order to give a sufficient reason – a complete explanation – for the existence of the cosmos, there must be something outside that cosmos. For Leibniz, there is only one such thing – a thing that exists of absolute necessity, and that is God. God, then, has two particularly important features: (1) He is the sufficient or ultimate reason for things and (2) He exists of absolute necessity.

---

[43] Leibniz (2017b), p. 1.

That God exists of absolute necessity is interesting for a number of reasons – reasons beyond merely establishing His modal status. First, God's necessity is derived from the thought that He must be unlike the things He needs to explain – the contingent things.[44] Second, God's absolute necessity is intimately tied up both in His independence and in His ability to serve as the sufficient reason for everything else. Third, and as the quote indicates, God's absolute necessity is also connected to God's containing the reason for His existence internal to Himself.

> we could never find in matter a reason for motion, let alone for any particular motion. Any matter that is moving now does so because of a previous motion, and that in turn from a still earlier one; and we can take this back as far as we like – it won't get us anywhere, because the same question – the question Why? – will still remain. For the question to be properly fully answered, we need a *sufficient reason that has no need of any further reason* – a 'Because' that does not throw up a further Why? – and this must lie outside the series of contingent things, and must be found in a substance which is the cause of the entire series. It must be something that exists necessarily, carrying the reason for its existence within itself; only *that* can give us a sufficient reason at which we can stop, having no further Why?-question taking us from this being to something else.[45]

Why are these aspects of God, and the reasons Leibniz provides for arriving at them, so important? Here we see in Leibniz's account of God the quintessential features of an ultimate explainer. Not only does God serve to provide the ultimate reason or ground for everything else but Leibniz also gives us reasons to believe that God *must* be independently existent. God's independence isn't simply some feature that God has by dint of being, well, God, but it is part and parcel of how God is apt to be the ultimate ground of everything else.

Before moving on, there is one final point of note. Leibniz's God is self-grounded – God contains the reason for His existence internal to Himself. For Leibniz, what this means is that God's existence is part of God's essence. In other words, God exists *because* it is in God's essence to exist. Many people think this particular aspect of God to be some combination of impossible and nonsensical. We can avoid entering into the fray of that debate and note only that it is Leibniz's commitment to the PSR that *partially* drives him to this conclusion. Why merely partially? Well, the pressure created by the PSR is such that *if* everything that exists has a reason for its existence, and God exists, then God must also have a reason for His existence. But, of course, this leaves open the

---

[44] On this Leibniz says, 'The reasons for the world, therefore, lie hidden in something outside the world, something different from the chain of states or series of things that jointly constitute the world' (2017b, p. 2).

[45] Leibniz (2017a), p. 3.

possibility that something *else* explains the existence of God, perhaps a Super-God. But if in order to be apt to serve as the sufficient reason for everything else God needs to be the end of the explanatory line, as per the quotation, then God needs to be the end of the explanatory line. The only way in which God can meet the demands of both the PSR and His office as ultimate explainer is if the reason for God's existence springs from God Himself.

2.4.3 Being

According to Heidegger, the central problem of philosophy is the question of being. There are peonies and trumpets, flamingos, hopes and numbers. What is this thing they have in common – their being – as expressed by the 'are'? That the formulation of the question involves the use of the copula – what *is* being? – should be our first clue that whatever the answer is here, it's not going to be easy. Heidegger, like Leibniz, is concerned to offer an ultimate explanation for the fact that anything *is* in the first place. Unlike Leibniz, however, Heidegger arrives not at the conclusion that God is the ultimate ground, but, instead, that *Being* is.

Legs and tops help explain the existence of tables, petals and stems help explain the existence of peonies. But for each new entity that we invoke, its being also needs to be accounted for. We are faced, then, with a familiar dilemma: in order to account for the being of entities, those entities must be ultimately grounded in something that is self-grounded (a loop), something that is ungrounded (an independent entity) or ultimately grounded in nothing at all, but a member of an infinitely regressive grounding chain. Although matters are exegetically very complicated here, we can be sure that Heidegger rejects the first and third possibilities. As far as Heidegger is concerned, what accounts for the being of entities cannot be self-grounded; nor can the being of entities be accounted for if they are members of infinitely regressive grounding chains.[46] What remains, then, is the second option.

Whatever ultimately grounds the being of entities must itself not need its being explained – lest we are forced off on a regress or into a loop. The ultimate ground of beings – Being – then, is ungrounded. But what kind of thing can be ungrounded? According to Heidegger, the only kind of thing apt to ground the being of entities – Being – cannot be an entity, because if it is an entity, then it has being, and if it has being, its being demands a ground or explanation. In order to ground the being of entities, Being must be ungrounded, without being and, therewith, not an entity.

---

[46] See Casati (2021).

The difficulties here are, of course many, and it is very widely held that Heidegger's solution to the problem of being is either nonsensical or paradoxical or both. After all, if Being is not an entity, how can it do any explanatory work at all? How can we even talk about it?[47] I shall avoid any further discussion of these issues but would like to conclude with two observations. First, Heidegger and Leibniz differ over what they take to fall within the scope of the explanatory target. For Leibniz it is the fact that there are any *contingent* things whatsoever that cries out for explanation. For Heidegger, on the other hand, it is *entities* in the broadest possible sense that stand in need of explanation. For Heidegger, the being of numbers, symphonies and concepts is as much in need of an explanation as is the being of flamingos, pianos and carrots. Second, like Leibniz, Heidegger recognizes that in order to meet the explanatory burden, whatever is to account for the being of entities must be of a radically different kind to that which it explains – it *cannot* itself have being. Were something contingent to explain the fact that there are any contingent things whatsoever, then it would be amongst the collection of things that stand in need of explanation. Similarly, if what grounds the being of entities were itself amongst the beings, then it too would need its being accounted for. Just as nothing contingent can ultimately ground the fact that there are any contingent things whatsoever, nothing with being can ultimately ground the being of entities. Although God seems like a remarkably different theoretical posit to Being, closer inspection reveals that, metaphysically speaking, they have many important things in common.

3 The Metaphysics of Fundamentality

We return now to metaphysical themes. What does something need to be like, metaphysically speaking, in order to ultimately ground or explain everything else? What kinds of things are apt to play this particular role? What is the fundamental level like? The questions here are many and I cannot answer them all. In this section, I survey some of the metaphysical themes most commonly associated with fundamentality in the literature.

3.1 Well-Foundedness

It is somewhat natural to imagine that *if* there's something fundamental, between whatever is grounded in that fundamental entity and the fundamental entity itself there are a finite number of steps: a monkey sits on the back of

---

[47] See Casati (2021) for a thorough discussion of the paradox of being as generated by one way of interpreting the problem of being for Heidegger.

a turtle that rests on the rump of the elephant who holds them all up. Pertinent to an understanding of fundamentality is an important concept: *well-foundedness.*[48]

It is not uncommon to hear philosophers describe grounding, or the reality that it orders, as well-founded. Indeed, it is not uncommon for the notion of well-foundedness to be understood as the central plank of metaphysical foundationalism. It is important to be clear, however, on what is meant by it. Suppose the fact that I exist is grounded in the fact that my parts exist and that fact is grounded in the fact that the parts of my parts exist, and so on. Suppose, now, that that grounding chain terminates in, say, facts about the existence of fundamental particles. Let's say that between the fact of my existence and the relevant ungrounded facts is a finite number of steps. Where every grounding chain is downwardly finite, we can say that grounding (or reality) is well-founded.

But one need not be committed to well-foundedness in order to be a metaphysical foundationalist. It is also possible that reality admits of *both* something fundamental *and* downwardly infinitely descending grounding chains. Consider Euclidean space, which is comprised of points and regions. The existence of each region is grounded in the existence of the points between which it is located, but it is also grounded in the existence of its subregions. The existence of the points is ungrounded, but as each region divides into subregions, every region is grounded. Thus, each region is grounded in something ungrounded – so a member of a finite grounding chain – but also grounded in something that is grounded – so a member of an infinitely descending grounding chain. On such a picture, there is something fundamental, in which each region is grounded, but there are also non-terminating grounding chains. The appearance of even a single infinitely descending chain entails the failure of well-foundedness, but it does not *necessarily* entail the failure of metaphysical foundationalism.

In what follows, nothing much hangs on this distinction. The example of Euclidean space provides us with one good example of a reason to think that well-foundedness should not be what the metaphysical foundationalist is aiming for, so I won't be assuming it.

3.2 Purity

Another metaphysical feature of the fundamental of note is that whatever is fundamental is *pure*. According to Sider (2011), the principle of purity says that,

---

[48] See Dixon (2016) and Rabin and Rabern (2016) for sustained discussions of what philosophers could mean when they talk about the well-foundedness of grounding.

fundamental truths involve only fundamental notions. When God was creating the world, she was not required to think in terms of nonfundamental notions like city, smile or candy … Suppose someone claimed that even though cityhood is a nonfundamental notion, in order to tell the complete story of the world there is no way to avoid bringing in the notion of a city – certain facts involving cityhood are rock-bottom. This is the story of view that purity says we should reject.[49]

As most proponents of grounding speak in the language of facts, purity can be adapted thus:

PURITY_FACTS: Fundamental facts involve only fundamental constituents.[50]

Perhaps the biggest selling point for purity is that it just *seems* correct. It seems odd to suppose that *if* God were in the business of *only* creating the fundamental stuff from which all else springs, that amongst those fundamental things would be cities. Moreover, purity also seems to bear an important connection to independence. Consider an *impure* fundamental fact, one that makes reference to something non-fundamental, such as [New York City is at a certain spatio-temporal location]. As this fact contains a derivative constituent, it is reasonable to suppose that this fact is at least partially grounded in some other fact or facts – given some plausible assumptions about the entities that constitute facts also forming a layered kind of structure that can be linked to the layered structure induced by grounding. Arriving at basic, fundamental facts that are not dependent on anything else seems to demand that the constituents of those facts are not dependent upon anything else either.

In spite of its intuitive appeal, philosophers present reasons to reject purity.[51] Perhaps the most oft-cited reason for rejecting the principle is that it has the effect that facts about what grounds what *cannot* be fundamental. In other words, the principle of purity entails that grounding is itself derivative. How so? Consider the fact that {Socrates} is grounded in Socrates. This is a grounding fact: [Socrates grounds {Socrates}]. What can we say of this fact, is it fundamental or derivative? Because both Socrates and {Socrates} are derivative, by PURITY_FACTS, this grounding fact *cannot* be fundamental. As all grounding facts will have at least one foot in the derivative, no grounding facts can be fundamental. Grounding, then, must be derivative. But this result also seems counter-intuitive. There is a sense in which exactly what we would expect to be written into the book of the world, as it were, is the relation that is

---

[49] Sider (2011), pp. 1067.

[50] See also deRosset (2013b), p. 6, and Rosen (2010), p. 112, for statements of versions of the purity principle.

[51] See Barker (2022) for an argument that purity is *false*.

doing all of this important structuring. If grounding is derivative, then not only is it not written into the book of the world but it must also be grounded.

3.3 A Free Lunch

According to Jonathan Schaffer,

> Armstrong makes crucial use of the notion of 'the ontological free lunch': 'whatever supervenes ... is not something ontologically additional to the subvenient, or necessitating, entity or entities. What supervenes is no addition to being'. In Aristotelian terms, there is a straightforward way to understand Armstrong: whatever is dependent is not fundamental, and thus no addition to the sparse base.[52]

For Schaffer, as with many others, it is a feature of reality ordered by the grounding relation that *non-fundamental entities are an ontological free lunch* – they do not incur an ontological cost. On the other hand – *fundamental entities are ontologically costly*. For Schaffer, though, derivative entities are additional *commitments*, but those commitments come at no additional cost. Others deny that derivative entities involve additional commitment at all.[53] Thus, we can draw a distinction between what it is to be committed to an entity and what it is to consider an entity costly (or not). One might think, then, that one of the great advantages of the grounding framework, and the positing of something fundamental, is it vindicates a picture on which there is a slim ontological basis that delivers all of the rest of it at no additional expense. A desert landscape, but more Dubai than the Sahara.

If the fundamental entities are our only costly entities, then there is an additional principle in the neighbourhood that we might also find attractive. Just as Ockham's razor says we must not multiply entities beyond necessity, Jonathan Schaffer argues that the *Laser* says that *we must not multiply fundamental entities beyond necessity*.[54]

But what does it mean to say that the derivative entities are an ontological free lunch? First, it must be specified that what seems to be at issue here is the ontological innocence of an entity relative to its *full ground*. Why? It is only by way of something's full grounds that that entity is delivered, as it were. From the fact that Socrates exists, we get the fact that {Socrates} exists – It, Socrates, guarantees its existence. But from the fact that P, we are not guaranteed the fact that P and Q. This is because of the fact that P only partially grounds the conjunction. In cases of mere partial grounding, we aren't simply delivered what is grounded at all. To arrive at the ontological innocence of all derivative

---

[52] Schaffer (2009), p. 353.   [53] See for example Cameron (2014), p. 100.
[54] Schaffer (2015).

entities, we must also assume that everything derivative finds a full ground in the fundamental. This is an interesting assumption that I don't think has received as much philosophical attention as it ought to. At the very least, it entails that some, possibly all, derivative entities are overdetermined. Why? Most, if not all entities have full grounds at the derivative level – consider Socrates and his singleton or the fact that P or Q – so if they are also fully grounded in the fundamental, then they have at least two full grounds, making them overdetermined. More will be said about this in Section 4.

Returning to our question, let us suppose that, like Schaffer, we take the derivative entities to be free, but committal nonetheless. So, to claim that they are a free lunch is *not* (necessarily) to be understood as entailing that we are not ontologically committed to them. Derivative entities exist and count amongst our ontological commitments – their cheapness is not parasitic upon their non-existence.[55] A better way of trying to get some purchase on what it means for something to be an ontological free lunch is to understand our commitment to that thing as being *built into* or *nothing over and above* our commitment to its full grounds. In committing to the existence of Socrates, for example, there is nothing more that we need to do or to buy, as it were, to be delivered of his singleton as well. What it is to be committed to the existence of Socrates *just is* to be committed to his singleton.[56]

Not everyone agrees, however, that the derivative is ontologically innocent. Nor do they agree that it is the Laser, rather than the Razor, that we ought to be working with. Jonathan Barker denies the ontological innocence of the derivative by arguing that what he calls the *ontological innocence thesis* entails a contradiction and, therefore, ought to be discarded.[57] Fiddaman and Rodriguez-Pereyra offer a number of arguments both to the effect that the derivative entities are not an ontological free lunch and that the Laser is not the preferable principle. I will not rehearse all of them here, but note that the authors point out that although, on the face of it, one theory can appear more virtuous than another by dint of positing fewer fundamental entities – helping to make the case that it is the fundamental entities that are theoretically weighty and not the derivative ones – it is not always clear which of the theoretical virtues is actually doing the heavy lifting. A theory, T1, with fewer fundamental entities than another theory, T2, may appear more virtuous than T2, but this is not because (1) the derivative entities aren't ontologically weighty and (2) the

---

[55] Existence talk is hard. The only thought that I wish to convey here is that to claim that derivative entities are an ontological free lunch *isn't* necessarily to claim that they don't exist.

[56] See Barker (2021), pp. 3–5, for a more detailed discussion of how to understand what it is to be an ontological free lunch.

[57] Barker (2021).

Laser is correct, but because T1 posits fewer unexplained entities. T1, it turns out, may be more virtuous because it is a more *powerful* theory, as it posits fewer entities without explanation and not because the derivative entities are free-riders with the Laser guiding our sensibility about the fundamenta.[58]

3.4 On the Aptness to Ultimately Explain

It is clear that being independent is not sufficient to render something apt to ultimately explain. In order to ultimately explain, independent entities must be connected to the rest of reality – or the relevant parts of it – in the right kind of way. In particular, the right kinds of connections need to be explanatory. That our independent entities must also stand at the tips of grounding chains is captured, in the contemporary literature, in the language of completeness. Put more metaphorically, though, the idea is that the fundamental entities provide the blueprint for the rest of reality, or are all that God needed to create. They are the seeds from which springs everything else.

But what kinds of things have philosophers thought apt to perform such lofty explanatory tasks? It's one thing to muse abstractly about the nature of fundamenta and quite another to understand what kinds of things are, or if there is anything that is, up to the task. In Section 2, I introduced some historically noteworthy accounts of ultimate explainers. I defended the idea there that those accounts could be understood as examples of metaphysical foundationalism. Those potentially controversial historic accounts aside, the contemporary literature offers several noteworthy examples of accounts of fundamenta.

3.4.1 Priority Pluralism

So far, all of the language that I have used to describe fundamentality has presented the fundamenta as being (1) in most cases many, and (2) down at the bottom. The idea that the grounding relation is involved with the mereological ordering is a central plank of theorizing about grounding. Indeed, we are often encouraged to get purchase on the notion of grounding by recognizing that wholes are grounded in their parts. Grounding would seem to track mereological composition (with wholes grounded in their parts), with stock examples of fundamental entities being various kinds of simples. In the language of facts, a standard picture of fundamental facts involves facts about the existence and nature of the really small stuff and the laws that govern it.

To hold a view according to which what is ultimately prior, what is fundamental, is the many is to hold a view known as *priority pluralism*. If the

---

[58] Fiddaman and Rodriguez-Pereyra (2018), pp. 343–4.

cosmos – contingent, concrete reality – is a mereological whole, according to the priority pluralist, whatever is fundamental is arrived at by tracking the mereological ordering downwards towards the bottom. Whether or not such fundamenta actually exist is a matter of debate, but the priority pluralist holds that *if* there is something fundamental, then it is many and downwards. As priority pluralism is generally yoked to physicalism, the idea is that our best physics will tell us what is fundamental.

3.4.2 Priority Monism

As one might expect, priority monism is related to priority pluralism. Neither view seeks to establish what exists. The priority pluralist does not deny that the whole, in this case the cosmos, exists. What they seek to establish is what is ultimately ontologically prior. Similarly, the priority monist does not deny that the myriad things exist. Instead, what their view commits them to is the belief that what is ultimately ontologically prior is the whole, the cosmos.

If the cosmos is a mereological whole, according to the priority monist, grounding tracks 'upwards', with the parts of the cosmos being ultimately grounded in the cosmos. The priority monist agrees with the priority pluralist that there is something fundamental. They also agree that the cosmos is a whole composed of parts. Where their view diverges from pluralism is over the direction in which the grounding relation runs. At least this much is true of the relation between the cosmos and its parts. The priority monist can concede that chairs are grounded in their chair parts and deer in their deer parts, but every part of the cosmos is grounded in the cosmos, rather than in its further parts.[59]

3.4.3 Middleism

According to the middleist, the middle levels are all the levels between the bottom-most and the top-most levels. They are the levels occupied by chemical, biological, economic and very ordinary objects, such as bicycles and alarm clocks. *If* the middleist is a metaphysical foundationalist, then they will believe that it is one amongst the middle levels that is foundational, populated by what is fundamental.[60] Entities at the levels above the middle level and entities at the

---

[59] The terminology 'priority pluralism' and 'priority monism' was introduced into the literature by Schaffer to describe views about fundamentality, the cosmos and the direction of priority. Strictly speaking, though, both views can be embedded in any number of positions provided that they capture what is fundamental – the many or the one – and the direction of (ultimate) grounding – towards the many or the one.

[60] Middleism is also compatible with anti-foundationalism. The middleist can hold that the middle level is the most ontologically prior, but deny that there is anything fundamental. Perhaps one ascends, descends or enters into a loop infinitely at the middle level.

levels below the middle level are ultimately grounded in entities in the middle. In creating the world, all God needed to do was to create the middle stuff – or some particular layer from amongst it. In creating people, for example, facts about biological, chemical, economic and social systems come for free. This view then sits as a counter-position to both that of priority pluralism – where what is fundamental is at the bottom level – and priority monism – where what is fundamental is at the top level. As a middleist, though, one can still choose between pluralism and monism: the middleist pluralist thinks there are a plurality of fundamental things at the middle level; the middleist monist thinks there is only one.[61]

Although this view doesn't get much of an explicit airing, it is important to recognize that it logically, metaphysically and conceptually coherent, and that it – or something in its ballpark – has noteworthy historic precedents. For the Aristotle of the Metaphysics, for example, it is primary substances – me and my horse – that are what is most ontologically prior.[62]

3.4.4 Essences

It is not uncommon for philosophers to suppose that what is fundamental are essences, or facts about essences. Perhaps the clearest articulation of why essences are good candidate fundamenta is offered by Dasgupta. According to Dasgupta, there is a threefold distinction between facts relative to the notion of grounding: (1) facts that are apt to be grounded and have grounds – derivative facts; (2) facts that are apt to have grounds and happen not to have them – brute or fundamental facts; (3) facts that are not apt to have grounds at all. Dasgupta argues that these three kinds of facts fall under one of two positions in a taxonomy of his own invention: *substantive facts* – (1) and (2) – and *autonomous facts* – (3).[63]

To understand the difference between a substantive and autonomous fact consider the following two facts – [the sky is blue] and [all bachelors are unmarried males]. The first fact looks like the kind of fact that cries out for various kinds of explanation – it is a substantive fact. Why is the sky blue? What does the sky's blueness consist in? The second fact, however, doesn't – it is an autonomous fact. One can wonder why we chose to use the word 'bachelor' to

---

[61] Bernstein (2021).

[62] Priority pluralism, priority monism and middleism are typically understood as views according to which what is fundamental is located at the bottom of a mereological ordering (particles), at the top of a mereological ordering (the cosmos) or somewhere in the middle (people). It is worth noting, though, that both pluralism and monism are also compatible with middleism; a view according to which what is fundamental are middle-sized goods is, strictly speaking, also a kind of priority pluralism, for example.

[63] Dasgupta (2016), sections 2 and 3.

describe an unmarried male, but there is nothing further to be said about why bachelors are unmarried men – it's just true by definition.

But what does this have to do with essences? Facts about essences are autonomous facts; they are facts that don't have and don't need further explanation. The fact that I am essentially such as to be human is a fact about which nothing more can be said. Dasgupta connects autonomous facts to essences and fundamentality by way of a version of the PSR: every substantive fact has an autonomous ground.[64] Facts about how mountains exist, what wars consist in, what it is to be Australian – substantive facts – all ultimately ground out in facts about essences – autonomous facts. Unlike the fundamental but substantive facts of other kinds of foundationalism, essences have the advantage of being seemingly non-arbitrary stopping points. On the one hand, they allow us to explain why things are thus and such a way without, on the other hand, themselves throwing up further questions that demand further answers in the form of grounds (which they just happen not to have).

4 The Epistemology of Fundamentality: Regresses, Virtues and Other Desiderata

By now, the reader should have some idea of what folks are talking about when they talk about fundamentality. But why think there is any such thing – anything fundamental – in the first place? In this section we come to a central aspect of the epistemology of fundamentality. I will sketch what I believe to be the most powerful arguments available in defence of fundamentality, some of their less-compelling counterparts, and some reasons to think the best arguments available leave room for the viability of anti-foundationalist views nonetheless.

4.1 The Regress Problem

Consider my wristwatch and the fact that it exists. What explains this fact? Obviously, there is a causal explanation for its existence – it was assembled in a factory in China. But although having been assembled by a robot in the outskirts of Beijing causally explains how the watch came to be, it doesn't explain everything that needs an explanation. Let us suppose that the existence of the watch is *metaphysically explained* by the existence of its parts – bezel, case, crown, hands and so on. So, in answer to the question, 'what grounds the existence of the watch?', one can reply with, 'the fact that the watch exists is grounded in the fact that its bezel, case, crown, hands, and so on exist'. From here, though, a next natural question arises: okay, but what grounds the existence of the bezel, case, crown hands and so on? It is not hard to see, now, that

---

[64] Dasgupta (2016), p. 384.

whatever we invoke to explain the existence of those parts will likely inspire us to ask a similar and further set of questions; and it would appear, then, that we are potentially off to the races. According to the foundationalist, however, races are no good – at least not the metaphysical kind – and it is important, thinks the foundationalist, to put a stop to them. In positing the existence of something fundamental, the regress is thankfully terminated.

Although intuitive and of illustrious historic pedigree, the regress problem is subtle, difficult and often splashed around as though what exactly is wrong with regresses is obvious. But it's not. Once we admit the possibility of *benign* infinite regresses, the question of what makes for the viciousness of a *vicious* infinite regress becomes particularly pertinent. Things are made even more complicated in the context of contemporary debates over grounding and fundamentality by the refusal, oftentimes, to commit to the kinds of principles and explanatory desiderata that appear required to get the regress problem going: the role the PSR plays in generating the regress problem for metaphysical foundationalism is a case in point.

Returning to the problem to hand, one can wonder what is so bad about the threat of looming regress. Why think that an infinite grounding regress is vicious?[65] One thought is that if the existence of my watch is explained by the existence of its watch-parts, which are then explained by the existence of their parts and so on *ad infinitum*, we haven't really explained the existence of the watch after all. To paraphrase Jonathan Schaffer, in such a case, the being of the watch is infinitely deferred and never achieved.[66] A subtly different concern does not deny that *something* about the watch's existence gets explained at each stage of the regress, but nonetheless holds that so long as the regress doesn't terminate, not everything that needs an explanation has one, or not everything that needs a particular kind of explanation has it.[67]

Let us try to better understand these possible reasons for thinking that there must be something fundamental. According to the first concern, where there is nothing fundamental, the being of something – in our case the wristwatch – is never accounted for. And this will be true, presumably, for everything. But why suppose this is the case? The worry here seems to be that in order to account for the being of the wristwatch, I must *first* account for the being of the bezel, and so on. And in order to account for the being of the bezel and the other parts, I must *first* account for the being of the parts of the parts and so on.[68] One way of

---

[65] See Bliss (2013) and (2019), Cameron (2008) and (2022), chapters 1 and 3, and Priest (2011), chapter 12.5 for some examples of discussion of grounding and viciousness.

[66] Schaffer (2010), p. 62.   [67] See Bliss (2019b).

[68] See Cameron (2022), chapters 1 and 3, for a really compelling discussion of this particular problem as a reason for thinking an infinite grounding regress to be vicious.

understanding this pull along the chain of entities seems to be driven by an underlying commitment to a kind of *inheritance principle*: each member of the chain derives its being from the entities at the level below and that being needs to be accounted for if it is there to be bequeathed to the level above. Where there is no end to this process, the being of the watch is never actually accounted for at all.[69]

I believe, however, that there are at least two reasons to think that this understanding of the regress problem doesn't quite hit its target – where that target is a reason to believe there must be something fundamental. First, one can challenge the assumption that in order for B to be fit to account for the being of A, B's being must *first* be accounted for by C. Consider for a moment how explanation works in other domains. In order to explain why my dog is sick, we can appeal to the discovery that he has a bacterial infection. Not knowing why he got the infection or how those bacteria came to be does not normally lead us to conclude that we haven't really explained why the poor beast is sick after all. And our inability to *first* say what caused him to have the infection in nowise diminishes the sense of explanatory success associated with identifying the presence of an infection. In general, although at each stage of the regress a new question or questions arise, it is not at all obvious why we are supposed to think that necessarily we must answer them *before* we can consider what is at the stage accounted for. Explanation, as we commonly understand it, doesn't work this way.

The second problem with this approach to the regress problem is the assumption that invoking the existence of something fundamental successfully dissolves it. If, as Schaffer proposes, it is the *being* of entities that needs to be accounted for, why suppose that the fundamental entities escape the scope of such a principle? In the context of the hunt for reasons to believe that there has to be something fundamental, it seems patently question-begging to suggest that there are just some things, namely the fundamental entities, whose being needs no explanation. Historically, at least, the difficulties here seem to have been better understood. God, in being *radically different* from the entities that He was invoked to explain, could be reasonably thought to fall beyond the scope of the principle. Heidegger's problems with Being also reflect an understanding of the tension – if Being is to explain the being of beings, then it cannot itself have being and must, instead, be nothingness. There is good reason to believe that if foundationalism is in the business of accounting for being, the whole view goes badly out of the gate.

---

[69] See Cameron (2022), chapter 3, for a slightly different but very compelling discussion of this point.

Let us turn, then, to the second way of understanding why an infinite grounding regress might be vicious. Recall that the concern here is that if the regress does not terminate, then not *everything* that needs an explanation has one or not everything that needs *a certain kind of explanation* gets it. Unlike the first understanding of the problem, this second approach does not deny that the regress produces some amount of, or a certain kind of, successful explanation. What exactly could be at issue here? Suppose that C grounds B and B grounds A. Although A and B (and possibly C) all have an explanation, perhaps what remains to be explained is something like the collection of A and B (and possibly C) taken together. Alternatively, let us suppose that although C explains B and B explains A, the explanations are somehow incomplete and, thus, inadequate.

Unfortunately, however, it is also difficult to understand what we are to make of these concerns in the broader context of grounding and the foundationalist picture. Let us first consider the thought that there is something left over that needs to be explained – perhaps the totality of A and B. One natural thought might be that although A and B have explanations, what is without explanation is some additional thing, namely, the totality A, B. Turning to the metaphysics of totalities, we can suppose that the relevant totality might be a set or a conjunction, for example. What we discover, however, is that the need to explain such a totality cannot be what motivates the foundationalist position, for in both cases the totality at issue *already* has its ground or explanation. Exactly what grounds a set are its members, so if A and B form a set {A,B}, then what grounds that set are those very members. There is nothing leftover that needs an explanation. Similarly with conjunctions (A,B) and their conjuncts (A and B).[70]

What remains is the suggestion that although A and B have explanations, those explanations are somehow inadequate. One way of understanding this particular concern is in terms of the idea that although B explains A and C explains B, those explanations are *incomplete*. But what exactly could this mean and why should we think it a problem? A distinction that might be useful here is that as drawn between *full* and *partial* grounding. Perhaps C and B merely partially explain B and A, respectively, and what A and B actually need are full explanations. Two thoughts: first, suppose for illustration that the existence of Socrates fully grounds the existence of {Socrates}. Proponents of the foundationalist view don't normally believe that having a full ground amongst the non-fundamental things vitiates the need for those fully grounded

---

[70] See Bliss (2019b), p. 365, for discussions of what grounds the relevant totalities in the context of arguments in defence of fundamentality.

things to be grounded by something fundamental. In other words, the foundationalist view is *not* that only non-fundamental things without full grounds at the non-fundamental level are grounded in something fundamental. Fully grounded entities stand as much in need of fundamental grounds for the foundationalist as does anything else. Second, even if we were to agree that everything must be fully grounded – and is, thus, incompletely grounded unless it is – from here we do not arrive at there needing to be something fundamental. The demand that entities be fully grounded, alone, doesn't get us to the existence of something fundamental.

Finally, it is not at all clear why we ought to find incomplete explanations obviously problematic. Consider an analogy with causation. That the milk spoiled because of a bacterial infestation is not normally considered a failure of explanation because it doesn't make appeal to the origins of the universe. In the case of causation, at least, we consider incomplete explanations to be perfectly good all the time. Of course, there may be additional reasons in the grounding case to think that our explanations must be complete, but an additional story will need to be told as to why that it is. It is worth also mentioning that the demand for complete explanations looks dangerously like it might beg the question. How so? If a complete explanation just is an explanation that makes appeal to something fundamental, then the insistence that entities have complete explanations just is the insistence that entities are ultimately grounded in something fundamental.

So, what of regress arguments in defence of fundamentality? Can they be salvaged? I think they can. Suppose A, B and C are all non-fundamental things. Where B explains A and C explains B, and so on *ad infinitum*, although every entity that we encounter along the way has an explanation, we may not yet have an explanation for everything that stands in need of one. In particular, we don't have an explanation for the fact that there are any derivative entities whatsoever. In other words, where the regress goes on indefinitely we cannot explain why there is anything derivative in the first place. But why is this?

In order to think about this better, let us spell out a version of an argument in defence of fundamentality.

(1) There is an explanation for the fact that there are any derivative entities whatsoever.

(2) No derivative entity can explain why there are any derivative entities whatsoever.

(3) Therefore, there must be something fundamental.[71]

---

[71] Adapted from Bliss (2019b), p. 369.

The reader might note immediately that this argument structure is already familiar to us. Line 1 gives us an explanatory target and line 2 an externality assumption. The argument fits the structure set out in Section 2 that will generate an ultimate explanation. Interestingly, the sub-argument for line 2 – the reason to believe that line 2 is true – involves appeal to an argument from vicious infinite regress. This is very often, although not always, the case with ultimate explanations: vicious infinite regresses are very often used to motivate the externality assumption.

In general, regress arguments get their legs by first assuming a particular explanatory target – some particular explanatory goal that is to be reached.[72] What the regress shows us is that where the regress is not terminated, that goal is exactly what cannot be achieved. As mentioned earlier, in the case of arguments in defence of fundamentality, one (bad) version of a regress argument might tell us that we need an explanation for, say, the totality of all dependent entities, and where there are infinitely downwardly descending grounding chains this is exactly what we are never able to explain. Note, though, that the recognition of an explanatory target is not yet to have a reason to think that any non-fundamental entity is not up to the task to hand. That we need an explanation for the fact that there are any derivative entities whatsoever does not *entail* that no derivative is available for the job. Crucial to the success of these arguments, then, is our second, externality, assumption. And it is only with this assumption in place that we can infer that there must be something fundamental.

The crucial question then becomes, why suppose that no derivative entity can explain why there are any derivative entities whatsoever? Suppose I find myself standing in the Rann of Kutch admiring the exquisiteness of the local (enormous) flamingo population, I wonder how such magnificent beasts came to be. One immediately supposes that the obvious answer here is that this particular flamingo population is the offspring of a previous generation of flamingos, and that previous generation of flamingos the progeny of the generation before them and so on. Of course, explaining the existence of particular flamingos in terms of their flamingo parents *is* perfectly and acceptably explanatory. It is very difficult to see how we could deny this. But where appeal to successive generations of flamingos seems to let us down is in terms of the answer to the question 'why are there any flamingos whatsoever?' But why is this? The principle that seems to be in operation in the background here is what is known as the *kind-instantiation principle*: no member of a kind can account for how that kind came

---

[72] See Bliss (2013, 2019), Cameron (2022) and Maurin (2019) for presentations of views that, although not quite in agreement with one another, converge on this particular point.

to be instantiated in the first place.[73] By the lights of this principle, if I want to know why there are any bicycles whatsoever, no appeal to any bicycles will allow me to understand that.

The best reason to think that there must be something fundamental, then, is because we need an explanation for the fact that there are any derivative entities whatsoever and no account of reality according to which there is nothing fundamental – metaphysical infinitism or metaphysical coherentism – can allow us to explain this fact.

4.2 Theoretical Virtues

Arguments from vicious infinite regress are the most powerful arguments we have in defence of the thought that there must be something fundamental. Although I believe we have compelling reasons to think they do not establish the conclusion for which they are commonly wielded, their strength is derived from their modal force. If an argument from vicious infinite regress succeeds, we have reason to believe that there *must* be something fundamental. I believe I am not alone in thinking that there are versions of regress arguments to the existence of something fundamental that work, although I disagree with the other voices in the debate over what, exactly, those arguments are. Regress arguments aside, though, a second kind of argument that has enjoyed attention in the literature are arguments from theoretical virtue. Although such arguments won't tell us that there has to be something fundamental, they can provide us with good reasons to think that it would be *better* if there were.

Making use of the theoretical virtue of *unity*, Ross Cameron argues that a theory of reality that posits the existence of something fundamental is more unified than a theory of reality that does not.[74] How so? According to Cameron,

> If we seek to explain some phenomenon, then other things being equal, it is better to give the same explanation of each phenomenon than to give separate explanations of each phenomenon. A unified explanation of the phenomenon is a theoretical benefit … if there is an infinitely descending chain of

---

[73] See Bliss (2019b) for a defence of this principle and the thought that regress arguments so understood are the only versions of the arguments in defence of metaphysical foundationalism that make sense. The kind-instantiation principle is adapted from Maitzen (2013, p. 260).

[74] Cameron (2008). It is worth noting that Cameron formulates his argument in the language of ontological dependence. In the early days of the explosion of interest in the notion of grounding and fundamentality, it wasn't uncommon for those working in the area to elide talk of ontological dependence with that of grounding. We could, then, assume that Cameron is guilty of this in this paper and that what he says here could equally well be formulated in the language of grounding. Alternatively, and perhaps more charitably, we can assume that Cameron means what he says, that he is talking about ontological dependence, but that by analogy the same can be said of grounding. In either case, it seems reasonable to suppose that Cameron's argument for the unity afforded by foundationalism can be cast just as well in the language of grounding.

ontological dependence … it is true that for every dependent x that the existence of x is explained by the existence of some prior object (or set of objects), but there is no collection of objects that explains the existence of every dependent x. This is a theoretical cost; it would be better to be able to give a common metaphysical explanation for every dependent entity.[75]

But how are we to understand the notion of unity here and why should we think that foundationalism offers it? The difficulties with Cameron's argument are, in fact, many, and I cannot rehearse all of them. Let us consider, though, what appear to be three obvious ways that metaphysical foundationalism could offer a unified explanation in a way that metaphysical infinitism does not: (1) there is a plurality of fundamental entities, a subset of which ultimately grounds some non-fundamental entity; (2) there is a plurality of fundamental entities that together ultimately ground some non-fundamental entity; (3) there is but a single fundamentum that ultimately grounds some non-fundamental entity. None of these options, upon closer inspection, however, looks particularly appealing.

Unfortunately, (1) runs the risk of looking gerrymandered. Suppose some non-fundamental x is grounded in f_1, which is fundamental, and some non-fundamental y is grounded in f_2, which is also fundamental. What (1) proposes is that x and y have a unified explanation insofar as they are ultimately grounded in $\{f_1, f_2\}$ and that this explanation is more unified than if x and y were grounded in, say, $\{w, z\}$, where w and z are not fundamental. Not only is it difficult to see how the 'unity' of the proposed explanation confers any kind of virtue, but also how it has any advantage over $\{w, z\}$.

(2), on the other hand, looks to present with a kind of relevance problem. x and y, according to this interpretation, have a unified explanation insofar as they are both ultimately grounded in $\{f_1, f_2, ..f_{n+1}\}$. Let us suppose that amongst the collection of f_ns is an electron in Paris. If (2) is the case, that electron serves as amongst my ultimate ground, amongst Pluto's ultimate ground and so on. Although the explanation looks unified in a particularly strong and important sense, it delivers a view that looks deeply problematic nonetheless. And finally (3), it might be thought goes badly out of the gate for it forces us to commit to something like the existence of God or the truth of priority monism.[76]

Additional arguments from theoretical virtue in defence of metaphysical foundationalism can be found in the literature. Bliss mentions the possibility of an argument that employs the notion of *power*.[77] Consider the world-view of the metaphysical infinitist: A is grounded in B, B in C and so on *ad infinitum*. The infinitist might be thought to have a theoretical advantage over the

---

[75] Cameron (2008), p. 12.   [76] See Orilia (2009), pp. 337–40.   [77] Bliss (2019a), p. 363.

foundationalist insofar as the infinitist doesn't leave anything out. A theoretical *cost* of foundationalism is its commitment to a realm of unexplained/ungrounded entities.[78] This cost might be worth paying, however, if there is some theoretical work to which the fundamental entities can be put. In particular, if it turns out that there *is* also something left out in the infinitist picture that *only* fundamental entities can explain, then foundationalism might win out in the virtues department after all. The regress argument developed in the previous section delivers us just such a virtuous picture of metaphysical foundationalism. Not only does the argument allow us to justify positing the existence of something fundamental on pain of vicious infinite regress – the regress is vicious because no non-fundamental entities can explain why there are any non-fundamental entities whatsoever – but it also provides a reason to think foundationalism more powerful than infinitism – the foundationalist can explain why there are any non-fundamental entities whatsoever whereas the infinitist cannot.[79]

It is not difficult to imagine additional possible arguments from theoretical virtue in defence of fundamentality. One can imagine that it is possible to at least make the case that metaphysical foundationalism is *simpler* than metaphysical infinitism or that it is more *elegant*, for example.[80] That said, I think it is also important to acknowledge that however these arguments are constructed, whatever our initial intuitions are regarding, say, the simplicity of fundamentality, things will be more complicated here than they might at first appear. Whilst it might seem obvious that foundationalism, in avoiding infinitely descending grounding chains, ticks the simplicity box, it loses out in terms of another kind of simplicity. After all, where the infinitist has one kind or category of entity – the derivative – the foundationalist has two – the derivative and the fundamental.

4.3 Taking Stock

I have discussed and dismissed several ways of using the regress problem to motivate metaphysical foundationalism. In spite of the deficiencies of many versions of regress arguments in defence of fundamentality, I believe there is a version of such an argument that works: there must be something fundamental because there is an explanation for the fact that there are any derivative entities whatsoever and no dependent entity, is up to the task. This argument provides us with reasons to believe that a certain kind of entity, namely a fundamental entity,

---

[78] Fiddaman and Rodriguez-Pereyra also mention this same costliness of fundamentality.
[79] See Bliss (2019a, 2019b) for a sustained discussion of these points.
[80] See Brenner (2023), for example.

is required to explain the fact that there are any derivative entities whatsoever. It is not the job of the fundamental to explain how Kevin exists or how the fact that the sky is blue obtains. The fundamental entities are in the business of ultimate explanations and are, thus, concerned with accounting for how things are *in their generality*.

Considerations of theoretical virtue certainly have a place in any discussion of arguments for and against fundamentality. But these arguments find their place downstream from having established the *possibility* or *impossibility* of the foundationalist view. Having independent reasons to believe that there is something fundamental, the view can be fortified by appeal to considerations of elegance, simplicity, parsimony and power.

5 Fundamentality: Some Misgivings and Its Alternatives

I think it is safe to suggest that metaphysical foundationalism is the default view amongst contemporary thinkers. I think it is also safe to suggest that it has been the dominant view in the history of the Western tradition as well. Perhaps unsurprisingly, though, the view is plagued with serious metaphysical and epistemic problems. In this, the final section of this little Element, I will survey some of the problems faced by the foundationalist view and introduce its alternatives.

5.1 The Trouble with Fundamentality

In spite of its illustrious history and intuitive appeal, metaphysical foundationalism is beset with problems. Many of these problems have vexed some of our greatest thinkers and formed the backbone of entire philosophical programs. God, for example, is a notoriously metaphysically troubled being. How can something that is so *radically different* to everything else and so *properly transcendent* give rise to or ultimately explain anything (let alone everything)? How can such a being create out of . . . nothing? How can language apply to this radically other transcendent being? How can anything be truly and properly independent? The list goes on.

The idea that there might be myriad ways in which there is something *wrong* with metaphysical foundationalism hasn't enjoyed a significant amount of contemporary attention. Philosophers have certainly noted that the reasons to endorse the view might not be nearly so compelling as often supposed, but the full spread of possible problems with foundationalism is underexamined. Here, I introduce two sets of problems for foundationalism. They are not the only ones, and possibly not the most interesting ones either, but they are problems deserving of our attention nonetheless. Both problems can be drawn out by focusing on the question of what exactly it is that the fundamentala are supposed to be doing? What work are they invoked in service to?

5.1.1 What Work the Fundamental?

In the previous section, I defended a version of an argument from vicious infinite regress to the conclusion that there must be something fundamental. In order to help motivate that particular account, I mentioned one rival account – Schaffer's – and presented reasons to think it didn't work. In this section, I consider again Schaffer's account as well as one proposed by Dasgupta. I also reexamine my own. Regardless of which of these three accounts is correct, they share some common potentially deeply problematic features.

Let us begin with Schaffer. Suppose that I am, and my being stands in need of grounding or explanation. Let's say that my being can be explained in terms of my parts. And those parts in terms of their parts, and so on. The worry that Schaffer sees here is this: if we don't stop this regress somewhere, then the being of me, my parts, their parts and so on is never *really* accounted for – it is 'infinitely deferred, never achieved'.[81] In other words, we must arrive at something fundamental – something whose being is not to be accounted for in terms of anything else – if my being, the being of my parts, and so on, are to have being in the first place. It is in terms of this fundamental thing(s) that my being is, then, ultimately accounted for.

For Dasgupta, on the other hand, what seems to be at issue is something much more general – not the being of me or the Pacific Ocean, but of how things *in general* turned out this way, presumably, rather than some other. It is a desire to answer the question 'good grief, how come it all turned out like this?'[82] that motivates fundamentality for Dasgupta. Being able to account for the existence of this thing here and that thing there – which we are very often perfectly able to do – doesn't completely satisfy a particular kind of curiosity, for even where we can answer the question, 'why does the Pacific Ocean exist?', we can still wonder why the world turned out to be such as to have oceans and mountains, and so on, at all.

Both Schaffer's and Dasgupta's arguments have us circling firmly in the territory of ultimate explanations. As we might expect, then, both Schaffer and Dasgupta must have explanatory targets in mind as well as assumptions in place that push them outside the collection of things to be explained (externality assumptions). Schaffer is keen to account for the being of particular things – tables, people and so on. He seems also to believe that the being of particular

---

[81] This would be the case were the world to be gunky.   [82] Dasgupta (2016), p. 382.

things cannot be accounted for in terms of other particular things whose being also needs to be accounted for. Let us capture these assumptions as follows:

S1(Explanatory Target): The being of particular things that have being needs to be accounted for.

S2(Externality Assumption): No being whose being also needs to be accounted for can account for the being of any other particular thing.

Dasgupta, on the other hand, seems to be of the view that although local matters of fact are perfectly able to explain other local matters of fact, what local matters of fact are not apt to explain is the big picture question, 'how did things turn out this way?'. And it is in order to answer this question, thinks Dasgupta, that we need something fundamental. Let us capture his central assumptions as follows:

D1(Explanatory Target): How things turned out this way needs to be accounted for.

D2(Externality Assumption): No non-fundamental thing can account for how things turned out this way.[83]

Recall the argument I defended in the previous section and the assumptions it contained:

B1(Explanatory Target): There is an explanation for why there are any derivative entities whatsoever.

B2(Externality Assumptions): No derivative entity can explain why there are any derivative entities whatsoever.

What can we make of these arguments? The first point of note is that all three arguments look to be relying upon some version or other of the PSR. The being of particular things, how things turned out this way, and that there are any derivative entities are all pieces of the world that stand in need of explanation. The being of particular things, for example, is *not* something that *doesn't* cry out for explanation. Moreover, in this particular case, the being of particular things seems to stand in need of some kind of full or complete explanation. The being of particular things needs a *sufficient* reason.

This observation is interesting for at least two reasons. The first such reason is that it is not uncommon for philosophers to disavow the PSR. Whether it's because they believe that quantum mechanics presents us with counter-examples or because they don't consider the principle compelling in the first

---

[83] In Dasgupta's vernacular this could be rendered as: no substantive fact can account for how things turned out this way.

place, the default setting amongst most contemporary philosophers is that the principle is bankrupt. The second reason is that the relationship between the PSR and foundationalism is strained – foundational entities, in not having explanations, run the risk of falling foul of the principle used to motivate positing them in the first place. Leibniz, for example, understood the perils here very well. He understood that the PSR gives us a reason to believe that the totality of contingent things stands in need of explanation, but he also understood that in wielding the principle, God fell within its scope as well. Leibniz accommodated the extension of the principle to God himself by rendering God self-explanatory. Foundationalist arguments that appeal to some version or other of the PSR very often face a dilemma: the principle used to get them to the existence of something fundamental needs either to be applied to the fundamental entities themselves – decimating the view – or a story must be told as to how the fundamenta can escape the scope of the principle in a non–*ad hoc*, principled manner. For Schaffer, the fundamental entities are just the kinds of entities whose being doesn't stand in need of explanation. Dasgupta offers a more sophisticated approach to the fundamenta by arguing that there is a subclass of independent facts, autonomous facts, which *don't have* and *don't need* explanations. These facts are facts about essences. On my own account, fundamental entities are the right kind (and the only right kind) of entities to explain why there are any derivative entities at all.

It is not clear to me, however, that Schaffer or Dasgupta avoid disaster. I think we can legitimately wonder why, once we're in the business of accounting for the being of things, the allegedly fundamental entities' being doesn't also cry out for explanation. Similarly, once we're asking why things turned out this way, rather than some other, I believe we can legitimately ask 'why *these* essences and not some others'? Or 'why are *these* essences as they are and not some other way'? Both Dasgupta's and my own version of the argument rely on restricted versions of the principle: every substantive fact has an autonomous ground and every derivative entity has an explanation respectively. Dasgupta's restriction looks to have the foundationalist conclusion baked into it and mine is trivially true, for what is a derivative entity if not an entity that has an explanation. Modifications of the principle have a track record of being problematic and *ad hoc*. One can wonder if all three of our arguments ultimately fail owing to their use of the PSR.

Quibbles with the PSR aside, one might also wonder if there is something just a bit off about the explanatory targets in the first place. Take B1. What exactly are we asking here? Are we asking for an explanation for something like the fact that there are derivative entities? If so, the explanation for this fact is actually pretty straightforward: it is just a general fact, and general facts are grounded in their particular instances. What grounds the fact that there are derivative entities is the fact that I exist, the fact that you exist, and so on. All three explanatory targets look reminiscent of the kind of explanatory projects that proponents of cosmological arguments were engaged in. These explanatory targets just look like variations on versions of the question 'why is there something rather than nothing?', and many consider these kinds of projects to be nonsensical, defunct or best handled by the empirical sciences.

The second cluster of problems for foundationalism as argued for above spring from the externality assumptions, and, in particular, how we can motivate them. Take S1, for example. Why should we believe it? What it is saying is that no derivative entity can account for the being of another derivative entity. But we use derivative entities to explain derivative entities all the time. Not only do derivative entities explain derivative entities, but they very often (possibly always) explain them fully.[84] My existence *fully* accounts for the existence of my singleton. There might be some special demand on metaphysical explanations, such that they must be *complete*, but whatever this completeness is, it needs to be (1) something different to fullness, for many derivative things have full derivative grounds, and (2) non-question beggingly motivated. D2 and B2 face similar pressures. Why can't the derivative things allow us to account for why things turned out this way? Why can't dependent entities explain why there are any dependent entities whatsoever? Answering these questions is actually much more difficult than intuitions suggest.

5.1.2 Overdetermination

Let us turn, now, to what I am calling the *overdetermination problem* for metaphysical foundationalism. So far, what we have seen is that finding a role for the fundamental is less obvious than much conventional wisdom would have it seem. In the vicinity, there is a second (and related) way of understanding a problem for the fundamental. Let us assume a version of fundamentality according to which *everything* is grounded in something fundamental. I don't intend anything dramatic here, but just the idea that metaphysical foundationalism is a view that pertains to both concreta and abstracta. Suppose, now, that my singleton is fully grounded in me and also in something fundamental. My singleton has two full grounds – me and something fundamental. Cases such as these will abound. Now consider for a moment how we commonly understand *causal* overdeterminism:

---

[84] There is no principled reason to suppose that it is not the case that all derivative entities have a full ground at the derivative level.

COD: some E is causally overdetermined if it has two distinct, individually sufficient causes, c_1 and c_2.

From here, I think we can reasonably understand what I call *metaphysical overdeterminism*:

MOD: some E is causally overdetermined if it has two distinct, individually sufficient grounds, g_1 and g_2.[85]

So far, the reader must understand that I have said nothing about whether such overdeterminism is problematic or not, and only offered a definition of when some grounded entity is *technically* overdetermined by its grounds.

It turns out that much will hang here on how we disambiguate the term 'distinct'. If 'distinct' is understood to mean *numerically* distinct, then any two full grounds will count as overdeterminers. If 'distinct' is understood ground-theoretically, then things look quite different. Let us suppose that two facts are ground-theoretically distinct just in case there are two facts, neither of which is grounded in the other, where there is no third fact that grounds both of them. By the lights of such a definition, some structures will count as involving overdetermination and others not. Recall priority monism, according to which the parts of the cosmos are ultimately grounded in the cosmos. Because any two parts of the cosmos will share a common ground, no two facts can be involved in overdetermining any further fact. Consider the fact that something exists. This fact is spectacularly overdetermined: it is overdetermined by the fact that I exist and the fact that the planet earth exists. Yet, this will not be the case for the priority monist.

Conversely, we have every reason to suppose that for the priority pluralist the fact that something exists will be overdetermined by the facts that I exist and that planet earth exists. Depending on the kinds of structures at issue and how the notion of distinctness is disambiguated, the fundamenta will be involved in overdetermining non-fundamental entities as well. It is enough that the reader recognize that such cases will also abound.

But why think anything interesting is happening here? After all, it is not uncommon for philosophers to claim that metaphysical overdetermination is obviously unproblematic.[86] One reason for thinking as much is that the fundamenta are theoretically costly entities. In not having explanations, their addition to a theory makes that theory more expensive. This cost might be a cost we are willing to pay, but regardless of the benefits, the addition of unexplained entities to a theory is an expense nonetheless. Where fundamenta are involved in overdetermination, we have derivative entities with full explanations at the 'cheaper' derivative level – cheaper because in having explanations they are

---

[85] Bliss (2023).   [86] See Dixon (2016), p. 450, for example, and Bliss (2023).

less theoretically costly – and full explanations at the more costly fundamental level. Not only do we have derivative entities with at least twice as much explanation, but we have entities with twice as much and *more costly* explanations. And I don't think it helps here to appeal to Schaffer's Laser and the idea that whatever is derivative is a free lunch. Regardless of how cheap derivative entities are, or how austere we are with our fundamenta, fundamental entities simply come at a cost and derivative explanations are explanations nonetheless. The explanatory superfluity generated by overdetermining fundamental grounds needs to be addressed.

One can only hope that whatever the fundamenta are in the business of – whatever explanatory role they are playing – it is different to the explanatory role that derivative full grounds are playing. If the being of my singleton or the fact of its obtaining is fully explained in terms of my being or the fact of my obtaining, what are the fundamenta needed for? Here we see a return to the aforementioned themes. Perhaps the fundamenta are needed to explain not the existence of this thing here and that thing there, but rather to ground some general fact about how things are or why things exist more generally, as already mentioned. Perhaps, instead, the fundamenta just explain things *in a different way* to how derivative entities explain things. So, while my existence fully grounds the existence of my singleton, it doesn't ultimately explain it. I'm not at all convinced that there are non–question-begging arguments for the need for ultimate explanations of ordinary entities – a point already mentioned – but if there are, then grounding looks to be *multivocal*. There are at least two kinds of grounding relations: grounding amongst derivative entities, grounding$_d$, and grounding by fundamental entities, grounding$_f$.

5.2 The Alternatives

Even for someone not convinced that foundationalism is significantly – if not fatally – flawed, it is still the case that there are two logically possible alternatives to foundationalism on the table: metaphysical infinitism and metaphysical coherentism.

Recall, again, Agrippa's Trilemma in foundational epistemology. Beliefs, if they are to be justified, are members of justificatory chains that either terminate in non-inferentially justified beliefs (foundationalism), go on indefinitely (infinitism) or go around in a loop (coherentism). A similar space of possibilities can be mapped out for foundational metaphysics. Entities can be members of grounding chains that ultimately ground out in something that is not grounded in anything (foundationalism), of chains that do not ultimately ground out in anything (infinitism) or members of chains that go around in a loop (coherentism).

Supposing that we can agree that both infinitism and coherentism are at least logically possible, we can nonetheless wonder if they are metaphysically viable.

5.2.1 Metaphysical Infinitism

Suppose the fact that I exist is grounded in facts about the existence of my parents, my parts and so on. And that those facts are then grounded in further facts – say, about my grandparents and my parents' parts, and so on. And that those parts are then grounded in further parts and so on *ad infinitum*. This is how the world looks for the metaphysical infinitist. The infinitist shares with the foundationalist in believing that the world is hierarchically structured: grounding is asymmetric, transitive and irreflexive. Where they disagree with the foundationalist, however, is in there being something fundamental. Metaphysical infinitism is a species of *anti-foundationalism*.[87]

Is metaphysical infinitism a viable view? Well, it is certainly logically possible and if anything that is logically possible is metaphysically possible, then metaphysical infinitism is metaphysically possible too. For anyone who does not believe logical possibility to be identical to metaphysical possibility, however, there is an additional question to be answered. Are there good reasons to think that metaphysical infinitism might not be metaphysically possible after all?

The most compelling arguments against the possibility of infinitism once again centre around arguments from vicious infinite regress: metaphysical infinitism is metaphysically impossible because it gives rise to a vicious infinite regress. Without once again rehearsing arguments presented in previous sections, let us go immediately to the central thought that leads the proponent of foundationalism to see trouble with infinitism. According to the foundationalist, where there is nothing fundamental, either (1) nothing is explained, or (2) something in particular is without an explanation, say, the fact that there are any derivative entities whatsoever.

There are very many strategies open to the infinitist to meet the foundationalist's objections. The infinitist might object that *of course* things have explanations regardless of whether there is a fundamental level. What business are philosophers, scientists, mathematicians in if not generating (non-fundamental) explanations? (1), the infinitist might retort, just seems mistaken. Perhaps a more charitable rendering of (1), then, doesn't package the foundationalist concern as one over explanations but, instead, as a worry over *ultimate* explanations: (1*) without something fundamental, nothing has an ultimate explanation. This, thinks the foundationalist, is a reason to reject infinitism. It is not at

---

[87] See Bohn (2018), Morganti (2015) and Tahko (2018).

all clear, however, that this helps the foundationalist. If 'ultimate explanation' just means 'explanation that terminates in explananda that do not themselves have explanations', then the foundationalist concern simply looks to beg the question.

More promising is for the foundationalist to target (2) – where there is nothing fundamental, something in particular, perhaps the fact that there are any derivative entities whatsoever, is without an explanation. In section 5.1, I presented several reasons to think there are things wrong with foundationalism so motivated. It is open to the infinitist, then, to block the foundationalist argument by appealing to problems with the argument. Perhaps the infinitist can deny the PSR, for example. Or perhaps the infinitist can reject the explanatory target in the first place. There is one further, novel argument open to the infinitist that I would like to expand upon.

Recall the argument defended in the previous section according to which:

B1(Explanatory Target): There is an explanation for why there are any derivative entities whatsoever.

B2(Externality Assumptions): No derivative entity can explain why there are any derivative entities whatsoever.

B3(Conclusion): There must be something fundamental.

I have argued that this is the most promising argument available to the foundationalist. How might the infinitist resist it? Let us begin by thinking about what might motivate B2. Why suppose that no derivative entity can explain why there are any derivative entities whatsoever? There are at least four possible reasons to believe this assumption: (1) the circularity objection, (2) the never-ending questions objection, (3) the same questions' objection, and (4) the kind principle.[88]

Taking (1) first. One reason to believe B2 is that no derivative entity can explain why there are any derivative entities on pain of circularity. If some derivative entity were to explain why there are any derivative entities whatsoever it would be amongst the collection of things to be explained, rendering that collection self-explanatory. This objection is, however, a non-starter. Consider the totality of derivative entities. Let's suppose that collection is a collection of facts that form a *superconjunction*. Exactly what grounds conjunctions are their conjuncts, so exactly what we would expect is the superconjunction of derivative facts to be grounded by the derivative facts that are its conjuncts. What about (2)? The worry here seems to be that if A is grounded in B and B in C and

---

so on *ad infinitum*, then for each new derivative entity that gets thrown up, we ask of that new entity 'and what explains this one?' It's not clear how to understand this objection in a non–question-begging manner. What it seems to be telling us is that never-ending questions are bad because they never end. At the very least, we need an independent reason to think that our explanatory chains must terminate (that isn't just a restatement of that demand). Moving onto (3), things start to look more promising. The thought here is that every time I ask of some derivative entity 'what explains this thing' and the response is 'well, this other derivative thing explains that thing' and I find this answer *dissatisfying*, it is because it hasn't really answered the question I am asking in the first place. Suppose I ask why Tim exists, and I am told it is because Tim's parents begot him. But suppose I respond to this by saying, 'okay, okay, I know how people get created, but what I really want to know is how there got to be any of us in the first place'. In this case, the march to infinity is bad because we are pushed along the regress by a persistent explanatory failure. We keep asking the same question because we keep getting the wrong answer.[89]

There is something to this, but it is important to ask why this is the case: why can't the fact that Tim, Tim's parents and so on explain the fact that there are human beings in the first place? Here we come to the crux of things, (4), and what we can call the *kind-instantiation principle*:

(KI) Where K is any *substantial kind*, you can't explain why there are any Ks at all by invoking only Ks, even if your explanation goes on forever.

Plugging this back into our earlier argument, we get:

B1(Explanatory Target): There is an explanation for why there are any derivative entities whatsoever.

B2(Externality Assumptions): No derivative entity can explain why there are any derivative entities whatsoever.

(a) (KI) Where K is any *substantial kind*, you can't explain why there are any Ks at all by invoking only Ks, even if your explanation goes on forever.
(b) Derivative entity is a substantial kind.
(c) Therefore, you can't explain why there are any derivative entities at all by invoking only derivative entities, even if your explanation goes on forever.

B3(Conclusion): There must be something fundamental.

This argument turns on, amongst other things, treating the term 'derivative entity' as denoting a substantial kind. What this means is that the term

---

[89] See also Bliss (2013) for an elaboration of this concern.

'derivative entity' behaves in the same way as terms such as 'cat'. Here, now, is where a space opens up for an objection: is the term 'derivative entity' a substantive sortal in the way that 'cat' is?

We can distinguish between substantive sortal terms and adjectival terms. Examples of the former are 'flamingo' and 'human being'; and examples of the latter are 'rambunctious' and 'chartreuse'. An intuitive test for distinguishing between the two is in terms of countability: I can count how many flamingos there are, but I cannot count the rambunctious; I can count the number of rumbunctious flamingos in my pond, or the number of their rumbunctious outbursts, but not the rumbunctious. Substantival sortal terms pick out kinds – flamingo, human being. They have associated with them determinate criteria of existence and identity such that we can pick out members of a kind, distinguish them from members of others kinds, recognize when they cease to exist and so on.

Philosophers such as Lowe and Thomasson have argued that not all sortal terms are *substantive* sortal terms.[90] There is a subclass of sortal terms that functions grammatically like substantive sortal terms but *not logically*. These terms are often called *dummy sortals*. To understand the difference between a substantive sortal and a dummy sortal, consider the following toy example. If asked how many things I got for Christmas, I would cast my mind back and recall that I received a watch and two records. The philosopher in me might snicker and quietly note that I actually received many more things than two, for I received a watch, two records, two record sleeves, two watch hands, one strap, and so on. A philosopher much cleverer than me would note that from here we can take things even further – there is the right edge of the watch strap, the countless molecules, the grooves of the record and so on. Christmas last year, it turns out, was particularly abundant.

What is interesting to note here is that it is not actually clear how many things I received. This is not because there are too many to count (even if that is true). Nor is it because some of the things might seem gerrymandered – the fusion of the watch strap and the edge of vinyl number 1. The problem is that it is not clear how many things I received because it is not clear what it is to be a thing in the first place. I can pick out watches, watch hands, bezels, edges, sleeves, bottom-sleeve-corners and grooves. What I cannot pick out are the plain old things. Of course, watches, bezels and grooves *are* things. But there are no things that I received for Christmas that aren't watches, bezels or grooves *first*. The 'first' here is not intended in a temporal sense, but in something more like an ontological sense. Something's *thinghood* is parasitic upon its falling under

---

[90] Lowe (2009), p. 26, and Thomasson (2007), 6.2, for example.

a substantive sortal term. This, then, is a reason to think 'thing' is a dummy sortal.

What does this have to do with the case for infinitism? It turns out, quite a lot. Suppose we are willing to concede that some of our sortal terms are dummy sortal terms. *If* 'derivative entity' is a dummy sortal term, then we can wonder if it has consequences for the question 'why are there any derivative entities whatsoever?' and, with it, our explanatory target: there is an explanation for why there are any derivative entities whatsoever. I believe that it does. If 'derivative entity' is a dummy sortal term, one possible consequence for our question and target is that they are *defective*: the question and our explanatory target are simply not picking anything out. We can ask why are there any bottle tops whatsoever because 'bottle top' is a substantive sortal term. But because 'derivative entity' is a dummy sortal, it doesn't pick anything out, in which case the question (and our target) is bankrupt. If the quest to explain why there are any derivative entities whatsoever is the best reason we have to endorse foundationalism, and that target is defective, then foundationalism doesn't look like it has legs after all. Of course, this doesn't get us to infinitism, but it does get us to *anti-foundationalism*, which is a start.

There is a second approach here, however, that I find much more compelling. Recall that I suggested earlier that there is no way to be a thing that is not first to be a watch, bezel, groove or so on. One way of understanding the relationship between 'thing' and, say, 'bezel' is that the term 'thing' acts as a *covering term*. We were first introduced to this notion back in Section 1. Just as when we use the term 'GROUNDING' we might be using it as a covering term for 'member-ship', 'parthood' and so on, when we use the term 'thing', we are using it as a covering term for 'watch', 'bezel' etc. If *this* is how we care to understand 'derivative entity' – as a covering term – then something very interesting happens with our explanatory target. To ask why there are any derivative entities whatsoever, then becomes the question, 'why are there any people, sheep, planets, and so on whatsoever?' or, in the language of facts, 'why do the fact that I exist, you exist, the sky is blue, and so on, obtain at all?' And, generally speaking, we know how to answer these questions. We know how to explain the fact that I exist, that you exist, or why there are sheep. And we do *not* need something fundamental to do it. The covering term conception of 'derivative entity' allows us to respect our explanatory target and supply all the explan-ations that we are after. Match point, it would seem, to the infinitist.

So, we have compelling reasons to think that it is not true that there must be something fundamental on pain of vicious infinite regress. This means that we have compelling reasons to think that metaphysical infinitism is metaphysically possible. Are there any other obstacles to the possibility of infinitism? No argument from theoretical virtue will deliver the possibility (or impossibility) of infinitism, but they will give us further reasons to find the view desirable or not. Depending on how the view is formulated, infinitism may well win points for its elegance and power. In contrast with foundationalism, which posits the existence of unexplained entities, infinitism is potentially a view on which nothing at all is left without an explanation, rendering it more powerful than its rival. These details, however, are to be worked out elsewhere.

5.2.2 Metaphysical Coherentism

We come, then, to coherentism. There are two desiderata on a system such that it might be considered coherentist: (1) it does not contain anything fundamental and (2) it admits of loops. Broadly, then, metaphysical coherentism, like metaphysical infinitism, is a species of anti-foundationalism.[91] Unlike metaphysical infinitism, however, it also denies that reality has a strictly hierarchical structure. Beyond these desiderata, coherentism comes in a variety of kinds. *Weak coherentism*, for example, holds that grounding is antisymmetric, transitive and non-reflexive. In a weakly coherent reality, grounding may well behave as it does for the foundationalist or the infinitist while allowing for some instances in which it loops. *Strong coherentism*, on the other hand, holds that grounding is symmetric, transitive and reflexive. For the strong coherentist, then, everything is grounded in everything else, including itself. But why entertain such madness?

The first reason to take coherentist pictures seriously is that people have advanced them. Consider this description of the worldview of seventh-century Chinese Buddhist philosopher Fazang:

> Far away in the heavenly abode of the great god Indra, there is a wonderful net which has been hung by some cunning artificer in such a manner that it stretches out indefinitely in all directions. In accordance with the extravagant tastes of deities, the artificer has hung a single glittering jewel at the net's every node, and since the net itself is infinite in all dimensions, the jewels are infinite in number. There hang the jewels, glittering like stars of the first magnitude, a wonderful sight to behold. If we now arbitrarily select one of the jewels for inspection and look closely at it, we will discover that in its polished surface there are reflected all the other jewels in the net, infinite in number. Not only that, but each of the jewels reflected in this one jewel is also reflecting all the other jewels, so that the process of reflection is infinite.[92]

---

[91] Not everyone understands coherentism as a kind of anti-foundationalism. Jan Swiderski (2022) presents coherentist models that are also foundationalist. I think that in order to occupy a horn of the Agrippa Trilemma – and thus to comport with coherentism understood as an *alternative* to foundationalism – coherentism cannot be foundationalist.

[92] Cook (1977), p. 2.

The picture presented here looks to be one of a strong coherentism. Supposing that we can understand this *reflection relation* as a kind of grounding, Fazang is claiming that everything is grounded in everything else. Why he believes this involves a complicated tour through his account of a certain way of understanding an identity relation – a tour that I cannot undertake here. More recently, Graham Priest has advanced a version of Fazang's cosmology according to which everything's dependence on everything else is mediated by a relationship to Ultimate Reality (emptiness). Although no doubt non-standard, the story as told by Priest renders the strong interconnectedness of all things less obviously false than the view at first sounds. But that is a tale for another day.

Strong coherentism, with few advocates and many detractors, is not a view that has gained a lot of traction. Weaker forms of coherentism look to be more readily available. At least, philosophers have argued that certain extant accounts look to entail the presence of grounding loops. In both set theory and mereology, non–well-founded sets and non–well-founded mereologies are well established. Ross Cameron has argued that certain accounts of sexuality and gender, mathematical structuralism and persons can be understood as kinds of *metaphysical holisms*.[93] And that the truth-teller and no-no paradox involve circles of ground.[94] Naomi Thompson is of the view that as explanatory holism is a viable position, and our understanding of metaphysical explanation is parasitic upon our understanding of explanation more broadly, then metaphysical holism (what I call coherentism) deserves to be taken seriously as well.[95] She also presents a slew of example cases of what appear to circular instances of grounding.[96] Carrie Jenkins also draws our attention to alleged instances of grounding loops. Jenkins points out that where brain states ground pain states and pain states are identical to brain states, we have instances of circular grounding.[97] Both Priest and I have argued that the north and south poles of magnets are grounded in each other.[98]

Obviously, example cases of a phenomenon give us reasons to believe that said phenomenon is metaphysically possible. Of course, it is always open to an objector to reject such accounts *because* they involve circularity. Broadly speaking, then, are there reasons to think there is something wrong with circles of ground?

Let us distinguish between what I shall call *large loops* and *small loops*. Large loops are loops such that A is grounded in B, B in C, C in D and D in A.

---

[93] Cameron draws a distinction between ontological dependence and grounding. Metaphysical holism is a view formulated in the language of ontological dependence for Cameron and not grounding, so perhaps my inclusion of these positions here is unfair.

[94] Cameron (2022), chapter 5.   [95] Thompson (2018).   [96] Thompson (2016 and 2018).
[97] Jenkins (2011).   [98] Bliss (2018) and Priest (2011).

In these kinds of loops, A appears in A's own grounding ancestry, but it is not necessarily the case that A grounds A. We can ensure this by denying transitivity. Small loops are loops such that A is grounded in A. In this case, we are dealing with a reflexive instance of the relation. The first point of note is that grounding circles of any size involve an infinite regress – only a regress that doubles back on itself. Anyone who thinks that infinite grounding regresses are vicious will likely think that grounding loops are similarly afflicted. Metaphysical coherentism, then, faces certain of the challenges faced by metaphysical infinitism.

To consider a further problem faced by large loops, let us imagine a time traveller case. Suppose I travel back in time and deliver a note to myself in which I detail instructions for building a time machine. Unable to resist the opportunity, past-me races to the local hardware store, buys all the necessary parts, enrols in a metalwork class at night school and sets about building the time machine. After a few false starts, and many years, it works and I travel back in time to hand to me the detailed instructions. What David Lewis notes in such cases is that we *do* have a series of perfectly good (causal) explanations here.[99] What explains my setting about building a time machine is my having received a very detailed set of instructions for doing as such. What explains my travelling back in time is my having successfully built a functioning time machine. What we have here is a causal loop – I have the instructions because I travelled back in time and gave them to myself – but it is one that generates a number of perfectly good explanations. What we don't have, though, is an explanation for how the loop got started. How did I come to know how to build time machines in the first place?! And as with the time traveller loop, so too with grounding loops. Large loops allow us to generate any number of perfectly adequate explanations – A because B, B because C – but what remains unclear is the question of how to break into the circle at all.

There are at least two ways one might respond to such a worry. First, perhaps there is an important disanalogy here with the time traveller case. The desire to explain how we break into the loop in the first place sounds like it is a question about temporal priority – and this concern simply doesn't carry over to the atemporal notion of grounding. In the grounding case, the problem might be better put as one of needing to explain the loop itself. The second response to this problem could involve either claiming that the question of what grounds the loop is somehow ill-formed or misguided, or that what explains the loop just are the members of the loop. This latter strategy involves treating the loop like a totality of some sort and then appealing to the thought that the metaphysics of

---

[99] Lewis (1976).

whatever kind of totality we have in mind is such that those kinds of totalities are grounded in their members.

So much for large loops – what about small loops? A small loop presents us with an instance of reflexive grounding – if A grounds A, then A is self-grounded. What might the problem be here? One thought is that being self-grounded is as good as not being grounded at all. As far as criticisms go, though, this is hardly an indictment of coherentism. At worst, it just turns coherentism into a species of foundationalism, which may come as a shock to its proponents but leaves the view no worse off than its rival. Another thought might be that it flouts our sense of ontological priority. If A grounds A, then A needs to come before itself in the ontological ordering. But it is not clear what the problem is here. Exactly what we would expect to be a consequence of a view that denies the hierarchical picture of reality is that it doesn't comport with the hierarchical picture of reality![100]

The most compelling reasons to think that small loops are a problem would seem to be explanatory. Let us suppose that the aim of explanation is to increase our understanding. One concern about small loops, then, will be that explaining something in terms of itself doesn't increase our understanding of that thing one dot. Put another way: how do we increase our understanding of something by appealing to the very thing that we don't understand such that we are seeking its explanation in the first place? One might worry, though, that this way of understanding explanation and how the understanding works presupposes a kind of linear model. Where we arrive at something that explains itself, do we not still come to understand *something* about that thing, namely, that it explains itself?

One final thought in defence of the acceptability of small loops draws our attention to an analogy with self-identity. Everything is self-identical, that's just what it is to be, but this self-identity is trivial. In this same way, then, we might consider being self-grounded to be trivial too. There is no further, metaphysically substantive story to be told about what it is to be self-grounded. It may even be a trivial consequence of some (or even all) instances of the grounding relation being symmetric in combination with transitivity.

5.3 Concluding Remarks

Metaphysical foundationalism is a stubbornly recalcitrant view. Not only has it been the default position throughout much of the history of the Western

---

[100] This is in contrast to the problem generated by self-*causing* entities. One worry here might be that something that is self-causing needs to exist *before it exists in time* in order to bring itself into existence.

tradition, but it has enjoyed a popularity in non-Western traditions as well. Indeed, schools that espouse non-foundationalist views are generally considered to be heterodox. In the more recent analytic exploration of grounding, fundamentality and the big picture metaphysics associated with them, philosophers have been known to justify their commitment to fundamentality with fleeting remarks about intuitions and pithy aphorisms. This is a real shame as, in my view, they do not do justice to the metaphysical richness and complexity of the view – the richness and complexity such that so many thinkers, the world over, have felt its pull.

One final word about ultimate explanations. Recall from Section 2:

ULTIMATE EXPLANATION$_{DEF}$: a natural or non-arbitrary stopping point (even if only a schematic one) to the nested series of available plausible explanations for increasingly general aspects of the world.

The biggest worry about anti-foundationalist views is that they may simply fail to meet the criteria of this definition, thus failing to deliver ultimate explanations. But look at the wording of the definition. It demands a *stopping point* to the *nested series* of available plausible explanations. The definition looks to be suggesting that the only way an ultimate explanation can be achieved is by way of a broadly foundationalist view. It is hardly a surprise, then, that neither infinitism nor coherentism fit the bill. Adjudicating between these three positions requires much more than intuition mongering and demands a broad consideration of basic principles such as the PSR and how we understand a very old, very big picture kind of explanatory project.

References

Amijee F., 'Principle of Sufficient Reason', in *The Routledge Handbook of Metaphysical Grounding*, M. J. Raven (ed.), Routledge (2020) pp. 63–75.

Barker J., 'Against Purity', *Ergo*, vol. 9 no. 50 (2023), p. 50. pp. 1381–1409.

Barker J., 'Grounding and the Myth of Ontological Innocence', *Australasian Journal of Philosophy*, vol. 99, no. 2 (2021), pp. 202–18.

Bennett K., *Making Things Up*. Oxford University Press (2018).

Bernstein S., 'Could a Middle Level be the Most Fundamental?', *Philosophical Studies*, vol. 178 (2021), pp. 1065–78.

Bliss R. L., 'Viciousness and the Structure of Reality', *Philosophical Studies*, vol. 166, no. 2 (2013), pp. 399–418.

Bliss R., 'Grounding and Reflexivity', in *Reality and Its Structure: Essays in Fundamentality*, R. Bliss and G. Priest (eds.), Oxford University Press (2018), pp. 70–90.

Bliss R., 'Fundamentality', in *The Routledge Handbook of Metaphysical Grounding*, M. J. Raven (ed.), Routledge (2019a), pp. 336–47.

Bliss R., 'What Work the Fundamental?', *Erkenntnis*, vol. 84, no. 2 (2019b), pp. 359–79.

Bliss R., 'Fundamentality', in *The Routledge Handbook of Metametaphysics*, R. Bliss and J. T. M. Miller (eds.), Routledge (2020), pp. 211–21.

Bliss R., 'Metaphysical Overdetermination', *Philosophical Quarterly*, vol. 73, no. 1 (2023), pp. 1–23.

Bliss R. and Priest G., 'The Geography of Fundamentality', in *Reality and Its Structure: Essays in Fundamentality*, R. Bliss and G. Priest (eds.), Oxford University Press (2018), pp. 1–34.

Bohn E., 'Indefinitely Descending Ground', in *Reality and Its Structure: Essays in Fundamentality*, R. Bliss and G. Priest (eds.), Oxford University Press (2018), pp. 167–81.

Brenner, A., 'Metaphysical Foundationalism and Theoretical Unification', *Erkenntnis*, vol. 88, no. 4 (2023), pp. 1661–81.

Brenner, A., Maurin A.-S., Skiles A., Stenwall R. and Thompson N., 'Metaphysical Explanation', in *The Stanford Encyclopedia of Philosophy*, E. N. Zalta (ed.) (2021). https://plato.stanford.edu/archives/win2021/entries/metaphysical-explanation/

Cameron R., 'Turtles All the Way Down: Regress, Priority and Fundamentality', *The Philosophical Quarterly*, vol. 58, no. 230 (2008), pp. 1–14.

Cameron R., 'Parts Generate the Whole but They Are Not Identical to It', in *Composition as Identity*, D. Baxter and A. Cotnoir (eds.), Oxford University Press (2014), pp. 90–107.

Cameron R., *Chains of Being: Infinite Regress, Circularity and Metaphysical Explanation*, Oxford University Press (2022).

Casati F., 'Heidegger and the Contradiction of Being: A Dialetheic Interpretation of the Late Heidegger', *British Journal for the History of Philosophy*, vol. 27, no. 5 (2019), pp. 1002–24.

Casati F. 'Heidegger's Grund: (para-)Foundationalism', in *Reality and Its Structure: Essays in Fundamentality*, R. Bliss and G. Priest (eds.), Oxford University Press (2018), pp. 291–312.

Casati F., *Heidegger and the Contradiction of Being*, Routledge (2021).

Cook F., *Hua-yen Buddhism: The Jewel Net of Indra*, Pennsylvania University Press (1977).

Corkum, 'Aristotle', in *The Routledge Handbook of Metaphysical Ground*, M. Raven (ed.), Routledge (2020), pp. 20–32.

Dasgupta S., 'Metaphysical Rationalism', *Nous*, vol. 50, no. 2 (2016), pp. 379–418.

Della Rocca M., 'PSR', *Philosopher's Imprint*, vol. 10, no. 7 (2010), pp. 1–13.

DeRosset L., 'No Free Lunch', in *Varieties of Dependence: Ontological Dependence, Grounding, Supervenience, Response-Dependence*, M. Hoetlje, B. Schnieder and A. Steinberg (eds.), Philosophia Verlag (2013a), pp. 243–70.

DeRosset L., 'Grounding Explanations', *Philosophers' Imprint*, vol. 13 (2013b), pp. 1–26.

Dixon T. S., 'What Is the Well-Foundedness of Grounding?', *Mind*, vol. 125, no. 498 (2016), pp. 439–68.

Fiddaman M. and Rodriguez-Pereyra G., 'The Razor and the Laser', *Analytic Philosophy*, vol. 59, no. 3 (2018), pp. 341–58.

Fine K., 'Guide to Ground', in *Metaphysical Grounding: Understanding the Structure of Reality*, F. Correia and B. Schnieder (eds.), Cambridge University Press (2012), pp. 37–80.

Fine K., 'The Question of Realism', *Philosophers' Imprint*, vol. 1 (2001), pp. 1–30.

Jenkins C., 'Explanation and Fundamentality', in *Metaphysical Grounding: Understanding the Structure of Reality*, F. Correia and B. Schnieder (eds.), Cambridge University Press (2012), pp 211–42.

Jenkins C., 'Explanation and Fundamentality', in *Varieties of Dependence: Ontological Dependence, Grounding, Supervenience, Response-Dependence*, M. Hoetlje, B. Schnieder and A. Steinberg (eds.), Philosophia Verlag (2013), pp. 211–42.

Koslicki K., 'The Coarse-Grainedness of Grounding', in *Oxford Studies in Metaphysics*, vol. 9 (2015), pp. 306–44.

Leibniz G. W., *Principles of Nature and Grace*, J. Bennett (trans.) (2017a).

Leibniz G. W., *The Ultimate Origin of Things*, J. Bennett (trans.) (2017b).

Lewis D., 'The Paradoxes of Time Travel', *American Philosophical Quarterly*, vol. 13, no. 2 (1976), pp. 145–52.

Lewis D., *On the Plurality of Worlds*, Blackwell (1986).

Lewis D., 'Ramseyan Humility', in *Conceptual Analysis and Philosophical Naturalism*, D. Braddon-Mitchell and R. Nola (eds.), MIT Press (2009), pp. 203–22.

Lowe E. J., *More Kinds of Being: A Further Study of Individuation, Identity and the Logic of Sortal Terms*, Wiley-Blackwell (2009).

Maitzen S., 'Questioning the Question', *The Puzzle of Existence: Why Is There Something Rather than Nothing?*, T. Goldschmidt (ed.), Routledge (2013), pp. 252–71.

Malink M., 'Aristotelian Demonstration', in *The Routledge Handbook of Metaphysical Ground*, M. Raven (ed.), Routledge (2020), pp. 33–48.

Martin C., 'Abelard on Grounding in Ontology and Logic', in *Grounding in Medieval Philosophy*, C. Normore and S. Schmid (eds.), Springer (forthcoming).

Maurin A.-S., 'Grounding and Metaphysical Explanation: It's Complicated', *Philosophical Studies*, vol. 176 (2019), pp. 1573–94.

Miller K. and Moron J., *Everyday Metaphysical Explanation*, Oxford University Press (2022).

Morganti M., 'Dependence, Justification and Explanation: Must Reality Be Well-Founded?', *Erkenntnis* vol. 80, no. 3 (2015), pp. 555–72.

Mulligan K., 'Austro-German Phenomenologists', in *The Routledge Handbook of Metaphysical Grounding*, M. Raven (ed.), Routledge (2020), pp. 90–101.

Normore C., 'Up in the Air: Buridan's Principled Rejection of Grounding' in Grounding in Medieval Philosophy, C. Normore and S Schmid (eds), Springer (forthcoming).

O'Connor T., *Theism and Ultimate Explanation: The Necessary Shape of Contingency*, Blackwell (2008).

Orilia F., 'Bradley's Regress and Ungrounded Dependence Chains: A Reply to Cameron', *Dialectica*, vol. 63, no. 3 (2009), pp. 333–41.

Paasch J. T., 'Ockham on Priority and Posteriority', in *Grounding in Medieval Philosophy*, C. Normore and S. Schmid (eds.), Springer (forthcoming).

Paseau A., 'Defining Ultimate Ontological Basis and the Fundamental Layer', *The Philosophical Quarterly*, vol. 60, no. 238 (2010), pp. 169–75.

Priest G., *Beyond the Limits of Thought*, Oxford University Press (2002).

Priest G., *One*, Oxford University Press (2011).

Pruss A., *The Principle of Sufficient Reason: A Reassessment*, Cambridge University Press (2006).

Rabern B. and Rabin G., 'Well Founding Grounding Grounding', *Journal of Philosophical Logic*, vol. 45, no. 4 (2016), pp. 349–79.

Raven M. J., 'Ground', *Philosophy Compass*, vol. 10, no. 5 (2015), pp. 322–33.

Raven M. J., 'Fundamentality without Foundations', *Philosophy and Phenomenological Research*, vol. 93, no. 3 (2016), pp. 607–26.

Raven M. 'Introduction', in *The Routledge Handbook of Metaphysical Grounding*, M. J. Raven (ed.), Routledge (2020), pp. 1–14.

Rosen G., 'Metaphysical Dependence: Grounding and Reduction', in *Modality: Metaphysics, Logic and Epistemology*, B. Hale and A. Hoffman (eds.), Oxford University Press (2010), pp. 109–36.

Roski S., 'Bolzano', in *The Routledge Handbook of Metaphysical Ground*, M. Raven (ed.), Routledge (2020), pp. 76–89.

Schaffer J., 'On What Grounds What', in *Metaphysics: New Essays in the Foundations of Ontology*, D. Manley, D. Chalmers and R. Wasserman (eds.), Oxford University Press (2009), pp. 347–83.

Schaffer J., 'Monism: The Priority of the Whole', *Philosophical Review*, vol. 119, no. 1 (2010), pp. 31–76.

Schaffer J., 'What Not to Multiply without Necessity', *Australasian Journal of Philosophy*, vol. 93, no. 4 (2015), pp. 644–64.

Sider T., *Writing the Book of the World*, Oxford University Press (2011).

Skiles A., 'Against Grounding Necessitarianism', *Erkenntnis*, vol. 80 (2015), pp. 717–51.

Swiderski J., 'Varieties of Metaphysical Coherentism', *Erkenntnis* (forthcoming).

Tahko T., 'Boring Infinite Descent', *Metaphilosophy*, vol. 45, no. 2 (2014), pp. 257–69.

Tahko T., 'Boring Infinite Descent', in *Reality and Its Structure: Essays in Fundamentality*, R. Bliss and Graham Priest (eds), Oxford University Press (2018), pp. 237–53.

Thom P., 'Ground in Avicenna's Logic', in *Grounding in Medieval Philosophy*, C. Normore and S. Schmid (eds.), Springer (forthcoming).

Thomasson A., *Ordinary Objects*, Oxford University Press (2007).

Thompson N., 'Metaphysical Interdependence', in *Reality Making*, M. Jago (ed.), Oxford University Press (2016), pp. 38–55.

Thompson N., 'Metaphysical Interdependence, Epistemic Coherentism and Holistic Explanation', in *Reality and Its Structure: Essays in*

Fundamentality, R. Bliss and G. Priest (eds.), Oxford University Press (2018), pp. 107–25.

Ward T., 'The Incoherence of Ockham's Ethics', in *Grounding in Medieval Philosophy*, C. Normore and S. Schmid (eds.), Springer (forthcoming).

Wilson J., 'No Work for a Theory of Grounding', *Inquiry*, vol. 57, no. 5–6 (2014), pp. 535–79.

Metaphysics

Tuomas E. Tahko

University of Bristol

Tuomas E. Tahko is Professor of Metaphysics of Science at the University of Bristol, UK. Tahko specializes in contemporary analytic metaphysics, with an emphasis on methodological and epistemic issues: 'meta-metaphysics'. He also works at the interface of metaphysics and philosophy of science: 'metaphysics of science'. Tahko is the author of *Unity of Science* (Cambridge University Press, 2021), *An Introduction to Metametaphysics* (Cambridge University Press, 2015) and editor of *Contemporary Aristotelian Metaphysics* (Cambridge University Press, 2012).

About the Series

This highly accessible series of Elements provides brief but comprehensive introductions to the most central topics in metaphysics. Many of the Elements also go into considerable depth, so the series will appeal to both students and academics. Some Elements bridge the gaps between metaphysics, philosophy of science, and epistemology.

Cambridge Elements ☰

Metaphysics

Elements in the series

Relations
John Heil

Material Objects
Thomas Sattig

Time
Heather Dyke

Metaphysical Realism and Anti-Realism
JTM Miller

Properties
Anna-Sofia Maurin

Persistence
Kristie Miller

Identity
Erica Shumener

Substance
Donnchadh O'Conaill

Essence
Martin Glazier

Truthmaking
Jamin Asay

Laws of Nature
Tyler Hildebrand

Dispositions and Powers
Toby Friend and Samuel Kimpton-Nye

Modality
Sònia Roca Royes

Parts and Wholes: Spatial to Modal
Meg Wallace

Indeterminacy in the World
Alessandro Torza

Grounding, Fundamentality and Ultimate Explanations
Ricki Bliss

A full series listing is available at: www.cambridge.org/EMPH

Printed in the United States
by Baker & Taylor Publisher Services